POWER-GLIDE
FOREIGN
LANGUAGE COURSES

Power-Glide Children's Spanish

Activity Book

by

Robert W. Blair

with

Dell Blair

This product would not have been possible without the assistance of many people. The help of those mentioned below was invaluable.

Editorial, Design and Production Staff

Instructional Design: Robert Blair, Ph.D., Dell Blair

Project Coordinator: James Blair

Development Manager: Erik D. Holley

Story Writer: Heather Monson

Cover Design: Guy Francis

Contributing Editors: Aaron Eastley, Erik D. Holley

Voices, Audiocassettes: Benjamin Blair, Dell Blair, Julia Blair, Robert Blair, Marco Lopez, Racquel Lopez, Mitchell Warner, Julia Young, Margaret Young, Robert Young

Illustrator: Apryl Robertson

Translators: Amiel Coco, Robert Blair, Dell Blair

Musicians: Geoff Groberg

Audio Recording, Editing and Mixing: Benjamin Blair, Geoff Groberg

© 1999 Power-Glide. All rights reserved.
Printed in the United States of America
ISBN 1-58204-031-1

No part of this publication may be reproduced, stored in a retrieval system, or transmitted, in any form or by any means, electronic, mechanical, recording, or otherwise without the prior written permission of Power-Glide.

Power-Glide Foreign Language Courses
1682 W 820 N, Provo, UT 84601

(7/99)

Contents

Introduction v
Adventure: In the Attic 1
Match and Learn 2
A Little Girl and a Rat 6
Adventure: Overboard, and to the Island! 17
Familiar Phrases 18
Adventure: Meeting Gabriela 19
Lines and Figures 20
Adventure: Talking on the Radio 27
Letter Codes 28
Adventure: Meeting Pablo by the Pond 41
A Boy and a Bear 42
Adventure: At the Market with Marcela 51
Colors at the Market 52
Adventure: Trek to the Middle of the Island 59
The Farmer and the Turnip 60
Adventure: Party with Javier 79
The Keys to the Gates of Rome 80
Adventure: Meeting Constancia 85
Body Parts 86
Adventure: Listening to Esmeralda's Story 99
The Broken Window 100
Adventure: Meeting Esteban at the Beach 125
Esteban's Challenge 126
Adventure: A Party of Friends 143
Pictograph Cut-outs 145

A Note to Parents

Basic Course Objectives

The major goal of this course is to get children excited about communicating in another language. The adventure story, the variety of activities, and the simplified teaching methods employed in the course are all designed to make learning interesting and fun.

This course is primarily for children pre-K through 4th grade. Course activities are designed specifically with these learners in mind and include matching games, story telling, speaking, drawing, creative thinking, acting, and guessing—all things which children do for fun!

Ultimately, children who complete the course can expect to understand an impressive amount of Spanish, including several common Spanish phrases, some complete Spanish sentences, Spanish numbers, colors, and body part words, and instructions for drawing and acting given in Spanish. They will also be able to understand stories told all or mostly in Spanish, to retell these stories using Spanish themselves, and to make up stories of their own using words and sentence patterns they have learned.

Children who complete the course will be well prepared to continue learning at a more advanced level, and they will have the foundation that will make learning at that level just as fun and interesting, albeit more challenging than in this course.

Teaching Techniques

This course allows your children to learn by doing: to learn through enjoyable experiences. The idea is to put the experience first and the explanation after. This is important to note because it is directly opposite to how teaching—and especially foreign language teaching—is traditionally done. Typically foreign language teachers spend the majority of their time explaining complex grammar and syntax rules, and drilling students on vocabulary. In this traditional mode, rules and lists come first and experience comes last. Learning experientially, on the other hand, simulates the natural language acquisition process of children.

When children learn their native languages apparently effortlessly in early childhood, it is not through the study of grammar rules and vocabulary lists. Rather, they learn the words for things around them simply by listening to others, and they intuitively grasp an amazing amount of grammar and syntax in the same way. By using activities that simulate natural language acquisition, it is not only possible, but normal for children to learn a new language quickly and enjoy doing it!

Specifically, this course motivates your children to learn Spanish by providing learning experiences in the form of matching games, story telling exercises, drawing exercises, singing and acting, and other fun activities aimed at developing functional language comprehension and speaking ability. These activities contrast markedly with the exercises in more traditional courses, which tend to focus exclusively on learning some vocabulary, or on understanding very simple Spanish sentences, without extending learning to the point of actually understanding and speaking the language. Significantly as well, the language your children will acquire through this course will be more useful to them than language learned through traditional approaches, because knowledge gained in fun rather than stressful ways is much easier for children to retain and much more natural for them to use themselves.

Using the Course

This course is carefully designed so that it can be used either by children working primarily on their own or by parents and children working closely together. Complete instructions, simple enough to be easily followed by children, are included on the tapes. However, to get the most out of the course, parents should use the thorough written instructions provided in the *Parent's Guide*. The *Parent's Guide* page or pages for each exercise state exercise objectives, provide instructions for students and teaching tips for parents, and give a full audio transcript. Using these helps, parents or other adults can enhance the course significantly by acting as facilitators: reviewing instructions, encouraging creativity and course participation, providing frequent opportunities for children to display what they have learned, rewarding effort and accomplishment, and providing enthusiasm. Keep in mind that much of the real learning takes place as you interact with your children during and after the course learning experiences.

Using the resources provided in the course book and *Parent's Guide*, an adult learning facilitator or *"maestri"* does not need to know Spanish or how to teach it in order to be a great learning partner. In fact, one of the most enjoyable and effective ways to learn is together, as a team.

Parents or other adults who know Spanish can, of course, supplement the materials in this course very effectively. A proficient bilingual *maestra* could, for example: (1) help children learn additional vocabulary by putting several objects on table and asking and answering questions about them, such as "What is this?" or "Where is the _____?", and so on; (2) create on-the-spot diglot-weave stories by reading illustrated children's books such as Silverstein's *Are You My Mother?*, putting key words (picturable nouns) into Spanish, and asking questions about the story or its pictures partly or completely in Spanish; (3) involve children in making and doing things (such as making a paper airplane or finding a hidden object) giving instructions all or partly in Spanish.

Benefits of Second Language Acquisition

Learning a second language has many benefits. Besides the obvious value of being able to understand and communicate with others, research in the United States and Canada in the 1970s and '80s has shown that learning a second language gives children a distinct advantage in general school subject areas. Seeing linguistic and cultural contrasts as they acquire a second language, children gain insight not only into the new language and cultures, but into their own language and culture as well.

Furthermore, a considerable amount of research has shown that learning a second language in childhood helps children learn to read and write their native language. Quite possibly the best phonics training a child can receive is to learn a language like Spanish, because Spanish spelling is quite phonetic: when one knows Spanish, the spelling of a Spanish word tells him or her how to pronounce it, and (with few exceptions) the sound of a Spanish word tells him or her how to spell it. This carries over to English and helps children intuitively understand how language works.

Our Goal

Our goal at Power-Glide is to change the way the U.S. studies language. We want to produce foreign language speakers, not just studiers. This *Children's Spanish Course* effectively launches children into speaking Spanish. We hope you and your children will find delight in the adventure of learning another language.

The Adventure Begins
In the Attic

Match and Learn
Point to what you hear

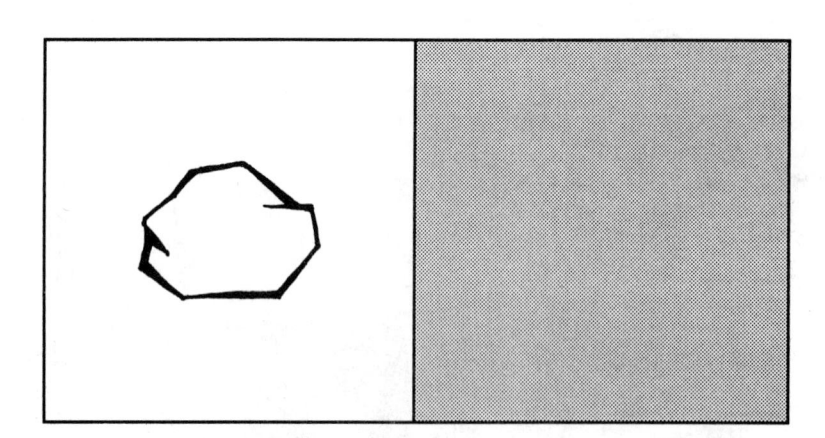

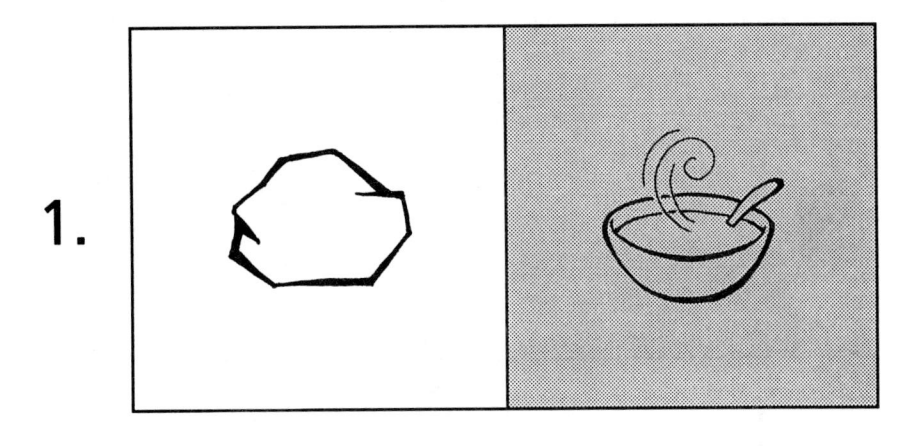

1.

2.

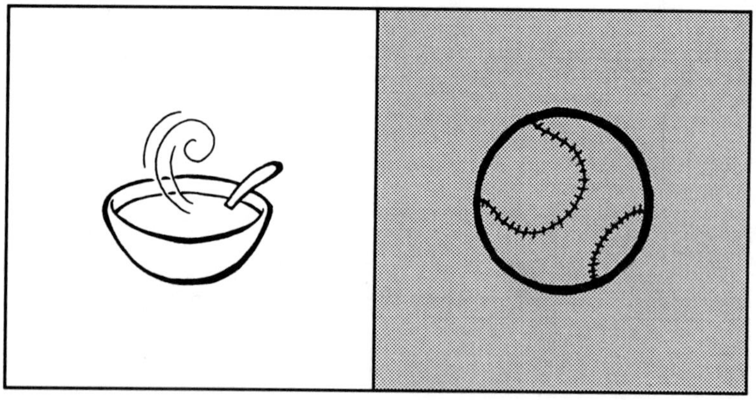

A Little Puzzle
Point to what you hear

Un Cuento
A Little Girl and a Rat

Match and Learn
Point to what you hear

1. 
2. 
3. 
4. 
5. 
6.

7

Match and Learn
Point to what you hear

1. 2. 3.
4. 5. 6.

8

Diglot Weave
Una Niña y Una Rata

Una 👧 sees *una* 🐀. *La* 🐀 sees *a la* 👧. *La* 🐀 squeaks "eek!" *La* 👧 squeaks back "eek!" *La* 🐀 runs. *La* 👧 chases *la* 🐀, but *la* 🐀 escapes. *La* 👧 sits down *y* laughs "hee-hee-hee." *La* 🐀 sits down *y* cries "boo-hoo."

Match and Learn
Point to what you hear

1.

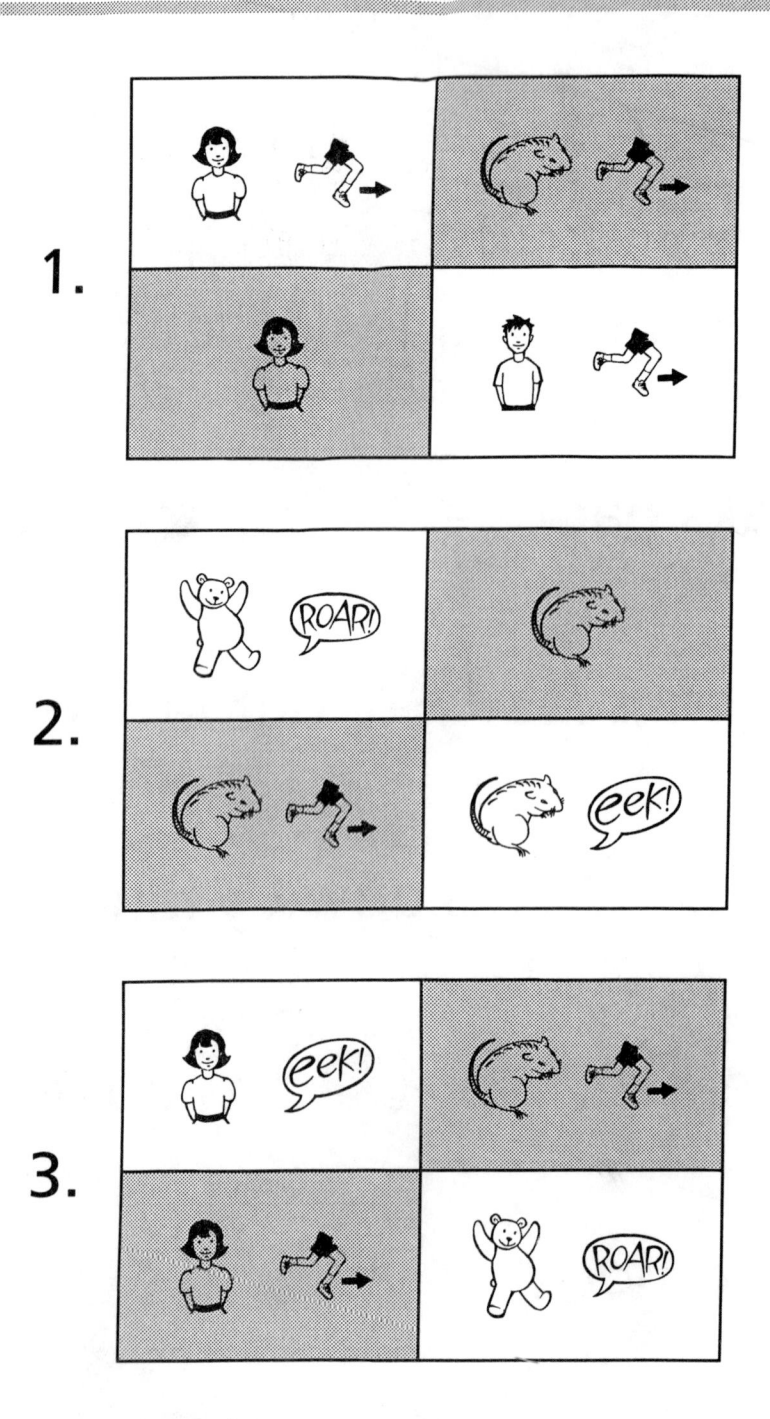

2.

3.

10

Match and Learn
Point to what you hear

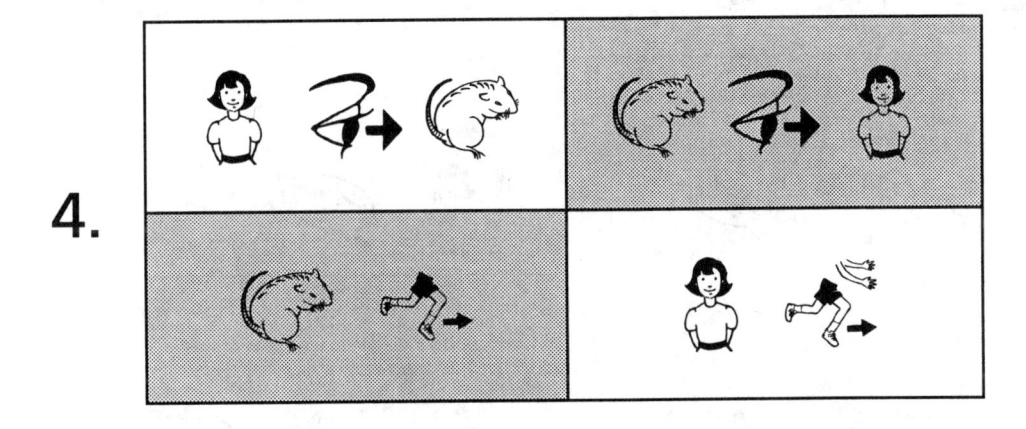

4.

5.

Rebus Story
Una Niña y Una Rata

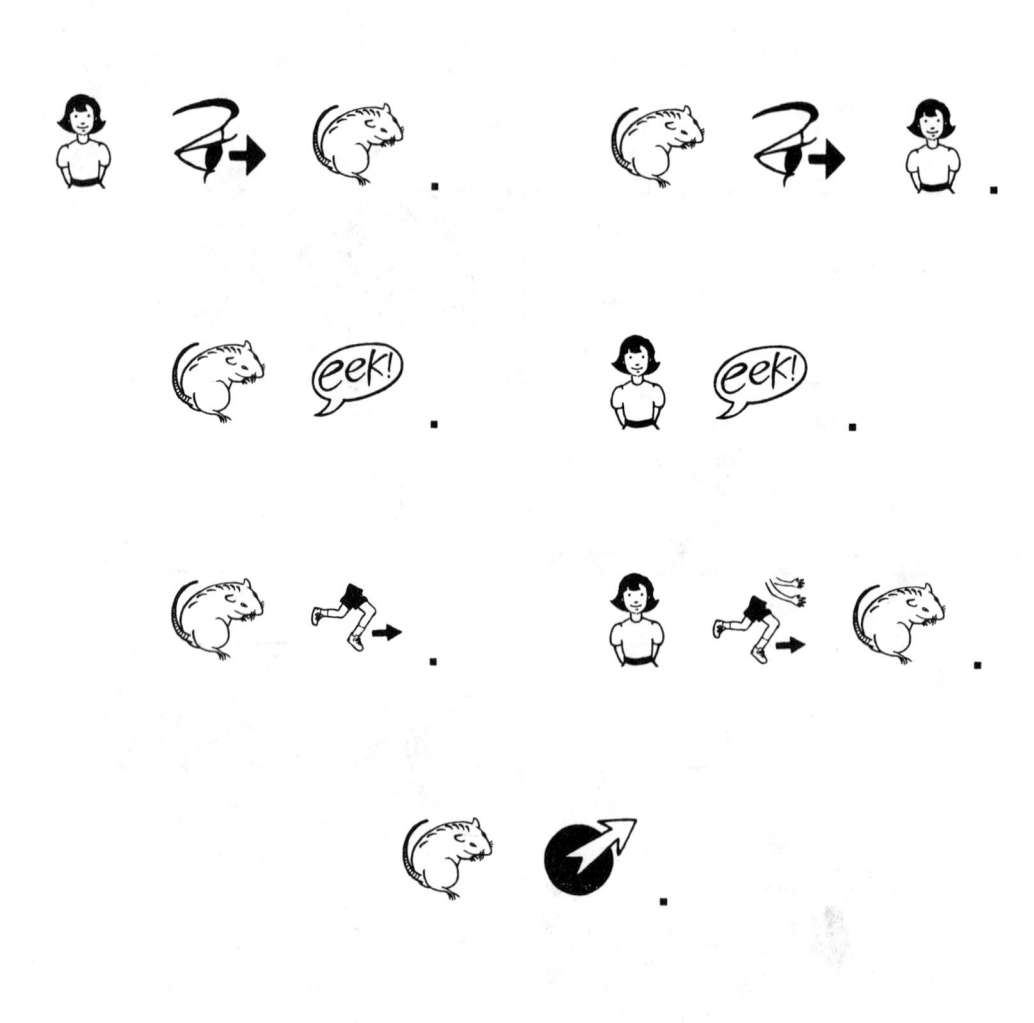

Describe What You See

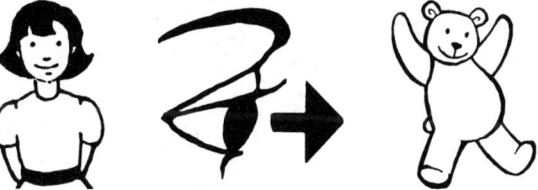

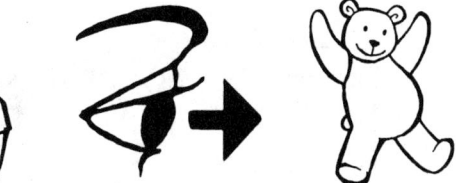

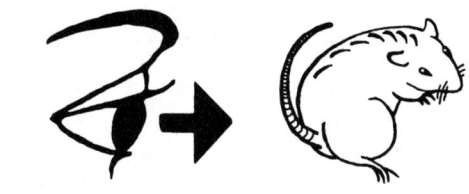

Story Telling
Look at the pictures and tell the story

14

Practice in Spanish
Listen carefully, then tell the story

Una niña ve una rata. La rata ve a la niña.

La rata chirría—eek! La niña chirría—eek!

La rata corre. La niña persigue la rata.

Pero la rata se escapa.

La niña se rie—hee-hee-hee.

La rata llora—boo-hoo.

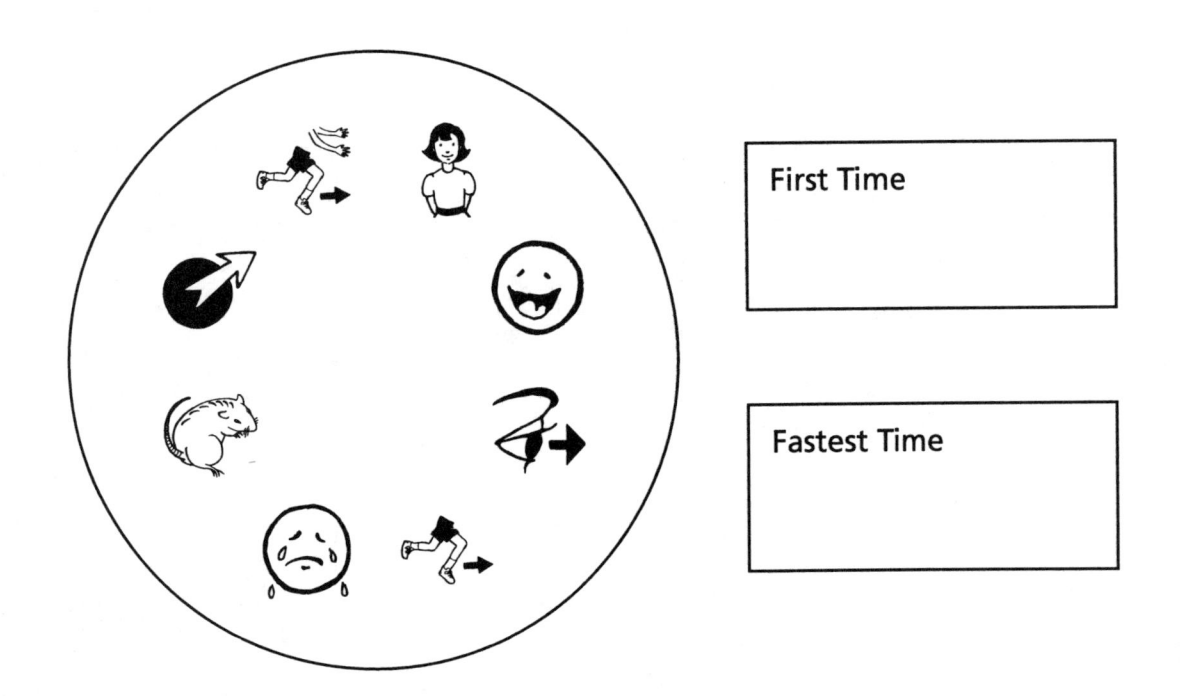

First Time

Fastest Time

The Adventure Continues
Overboard, and to the Island!

Familiar Phrases

1. *Hola.* — Hello.

2. *Buenos días.* — Good day.

3. *Buenas tardes.* — Good afternoon.

4. *Buenas noches.* — Good night.

5. *Me llamo* Glen. — I'm called Glen.

6. *Mi nombre es* Elaine. — My name is Elaine.

7. *¿Cuál es su nombre?* — What is your name?

8. *¿Cómo se llama?* — What are you called?

9. *Mucho gusto.* — Nice to meet you.

10. *Chao.* — Goodbye.

The Adventure Continues
Meeting Gabriela

Scatter Chart
Point to what you hear

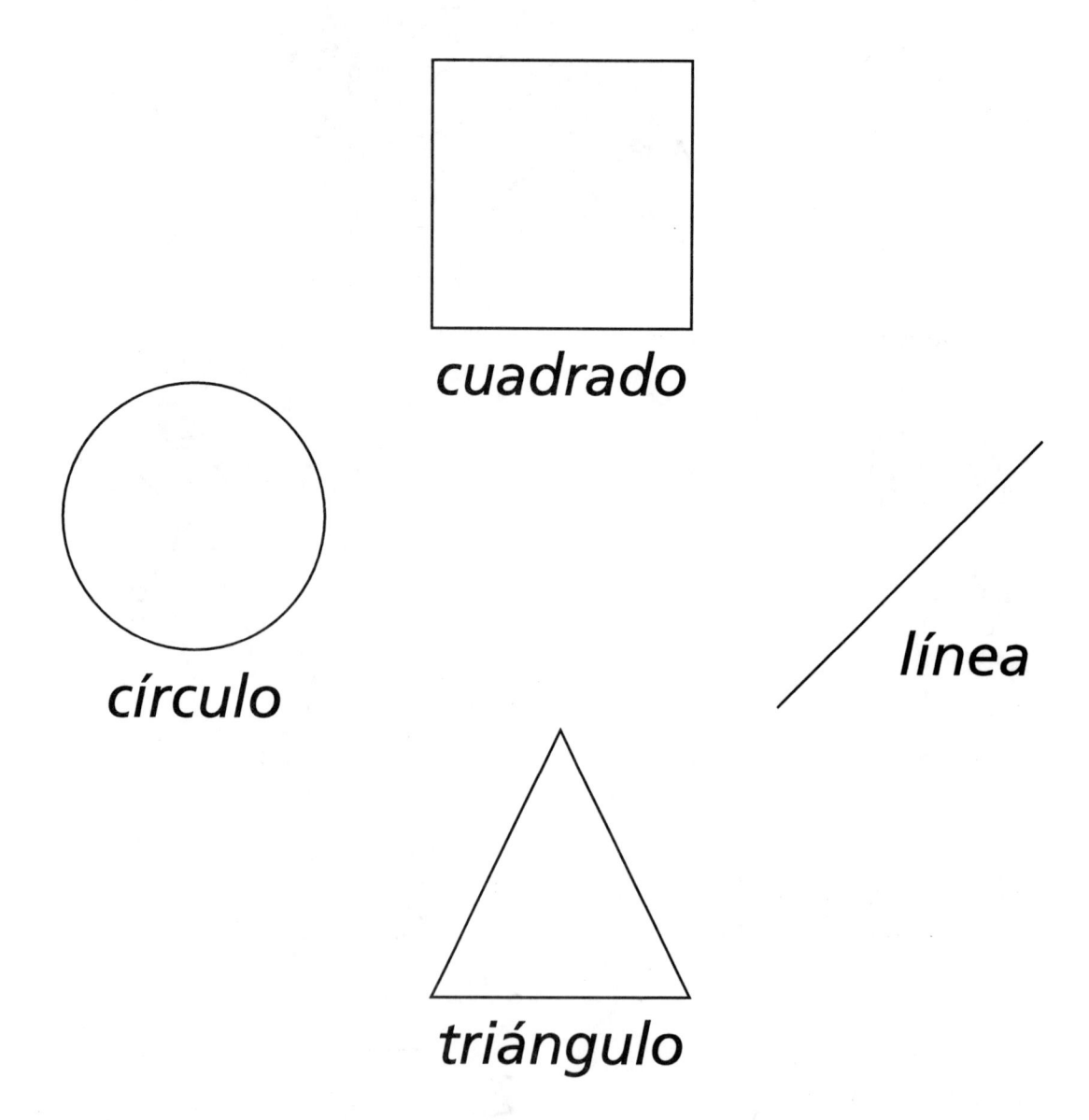

cuadrado

círculo

línea

triángulo

Look and Listen

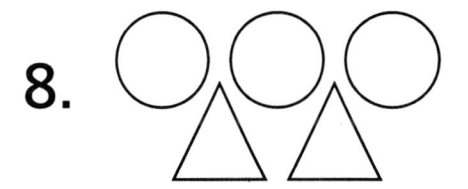

1. ○

2. □

3. △

4. /

5. △□

6. ○△

7. ○○

8. ○○○ △△

9. □□ ///

10. ○○△

11. /// ○

12. □□ /

21

Look and Listen Again

1. ○
2. □
3. △
4. ╱
5. △□
6. ○△

7. ○○
8. ○○○ △△
9. □□ ╱╱╱
10. ○○△
11. ╱╱╱ ○
12. □□ ╱

Match and Learn
Point to what you hear

1. 
2. 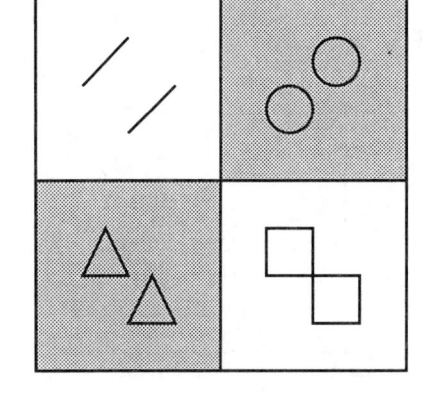
3. 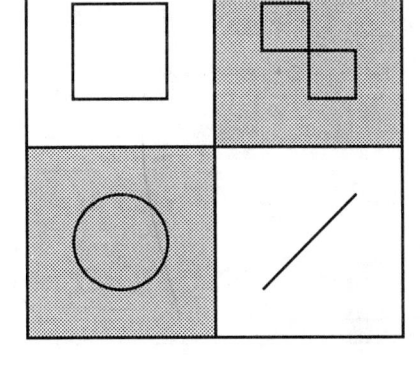
4. 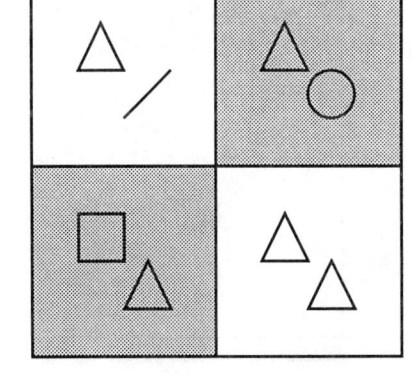
5. 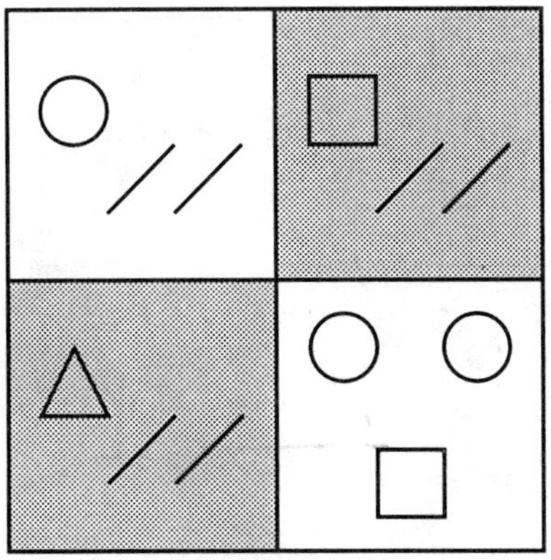
6.

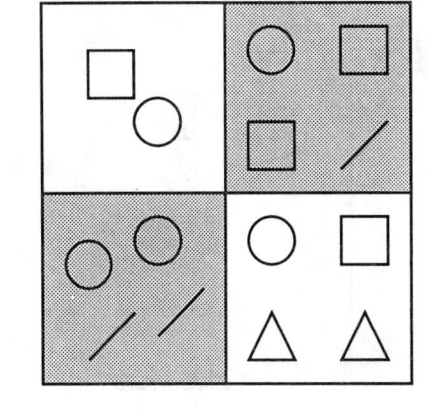

Listen and Draw

1.

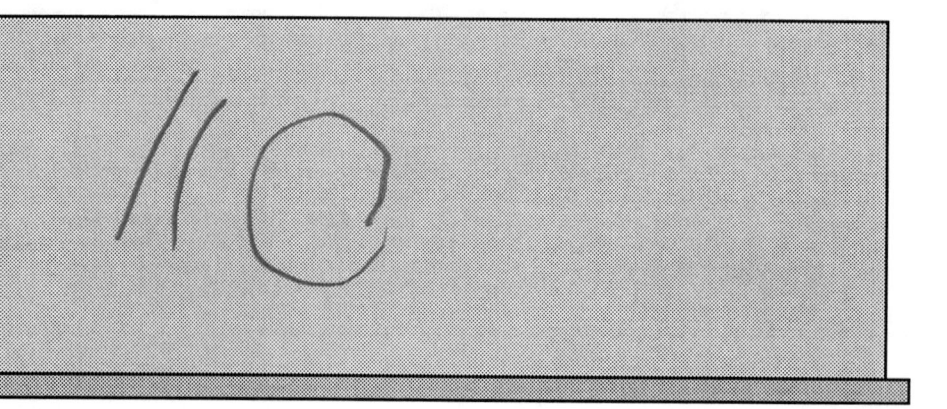

2.

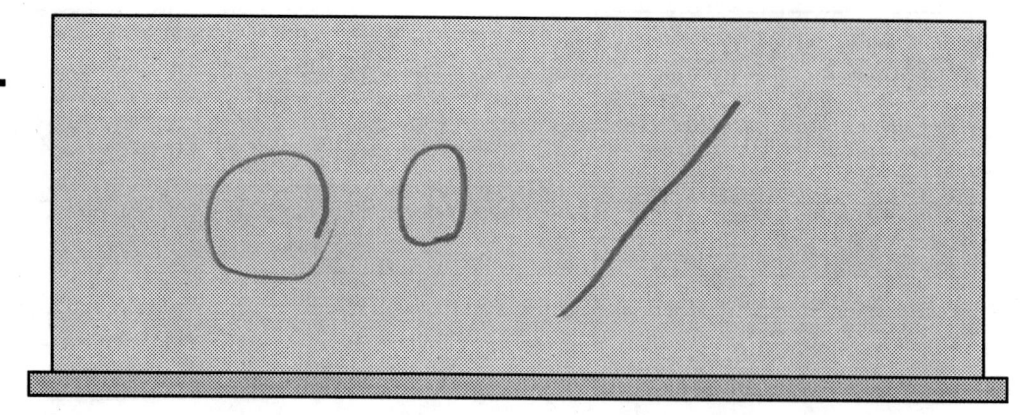

3.

Listen and Draw

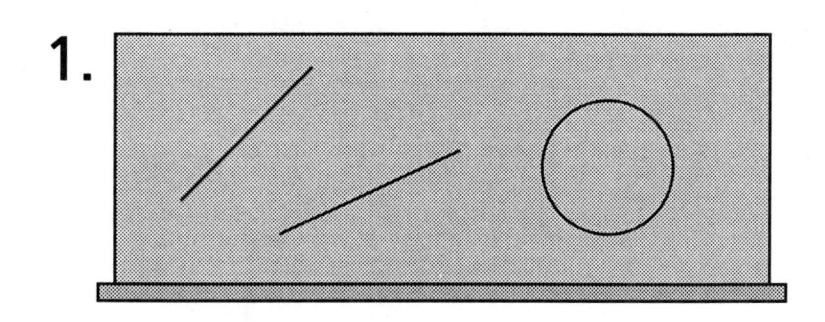

1. *Dos líneas y un círculo.*

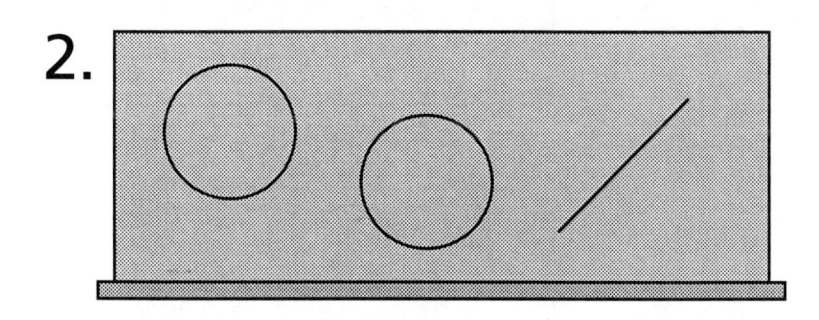

2. *Dos círculos y una línea.*

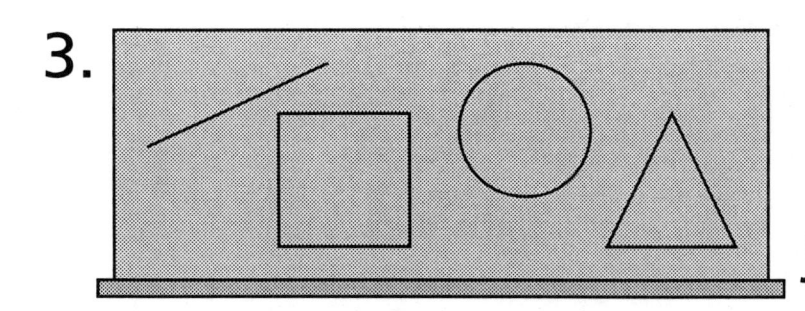

3. *Una línea, un cuadrado, un círculo, y un triángulo.*

Look and Say

1. ○
2. □
3.  △
4.  ／

5. 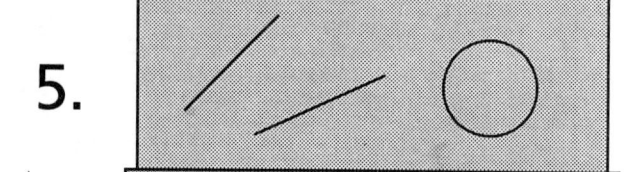 ／ ／ ○
6. 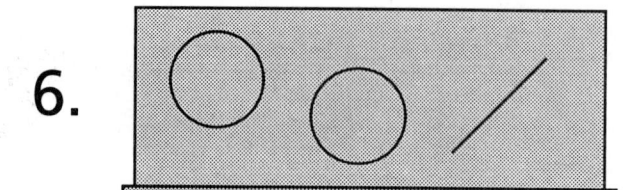 ○ ○ ／
7. 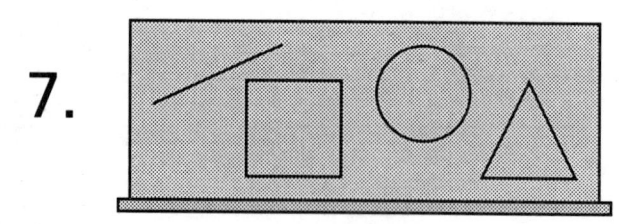 ／ □ ○ △

26

The Adventure Continues
Talking on the Radio

Letter Code Sentences

1. K S S-O?

2. S-O S ☐.

3. E K S S-O?

4. S-O S ☐, no?

5. C S-O S ☐.

6. E S-O S ☐.

🔊 Letter Codes and Words

1.　K　　S　　S-O?

¿Qué　es　eso?

What　is　that?

🔊 Letter Codes and Words

2. S-O   S   T.

Eso   es   sopa.

That   is   soup.

🔊 Letter Codes and Words

3. E K S S-O?

¿Y qué es eso?

And what is that?

Letter Codes and Words

4. S-O S ▢ ,   no?

Eso es sopa,   ¿no?

That is soup, isn't it?

Letter Codes and Words

5. C   S-O   S   C .

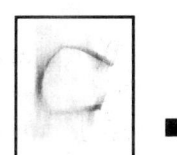

Sí, eso es sopa.

Yes, that is soup.

🔊 **Letter Codes and Words**

6. E S-O S ▢.

Y eso es té.

And that is tea.

Letter Code Meanings

C   (si)   = yes

E   (y)   = and

K   (que)   = what

S   (es)   = is

S-O   (eso)   = that

Letter Code Test

1. C　　(si)　　= _____

2. E　　(y)　　= _____

3. K　　(que)　= _____

4. S　　(es)　　= _____

5. S-O　(eso)　= _____

Letter Code Sentence Review

1. K   S   S-O?

¿Qué   es   eso?

What   is   that?

2. S-O   S   sopa.

Eso   es   sopa.

That   is   soup.

3. E   K   S   S-O?

¿Y   qué   es   eso?

And   what   is   that?

> **Letter Code Sentence Review**

4. S-O S té, no?

Eso es té, ¿no?

That is tea, isn't it?

5. C S-O S té.

Sí, eso es té.

Yes, that is tea.

6. E S-O S agua.

Y eso es agua.

And that is water.

Spanish to English

1. ¿Qué es eso? _____

2. Eso es sopa. _____

3. Y eso, ¿qué es eso? _____

4. Eso es agua, ¿no? _____

5. No, eso es té. _____

6. ¿Y es eso té? _____

7. Sí, eso es té. _____

English to Spanish

#10

1. That is water, isn't it?

   _____

2. No, that is soup.

   _____

3. And that, what is that?

   _____

4. Is that tea?

   _____

5. Yes, that is tea.

   _____

Week days
Months
Seasons

🔊 #11 The Adventure Continues
Meeting Pablo by the Pond

agua fresca
pescando

El verano me gusta por los días solanos
El Atono   festivas
El invierno
La primavera

41

🔊 #12

Un Cuento
A Boy and a Bear

Match and Learn
Point to what you hear

#13

1. 
2. 
3. 
4. 
5. 
6.

43

Diglot Weave
Encuentro Peligroso

Un 🧑 sees un 🐻. El 🐻 sees el 🧑.

El 🐻 roars—rrr! El 🧑 roars—rrr!.

El 🐻 advances toward el 🧑,

roaring—rrr! El 🧑 advances toward

el 🐻, roaring—rrr! El 🐻 hesitates,

then turns back and runs. El 🧑

doesn't hesitate. El 🧑 chases el 🐻.

But el 🐻 escapes.

El 🧑 🪑 y 😀. El 🐻 🪑 y 😢.

Match and Learn
Point to what you hear

1.

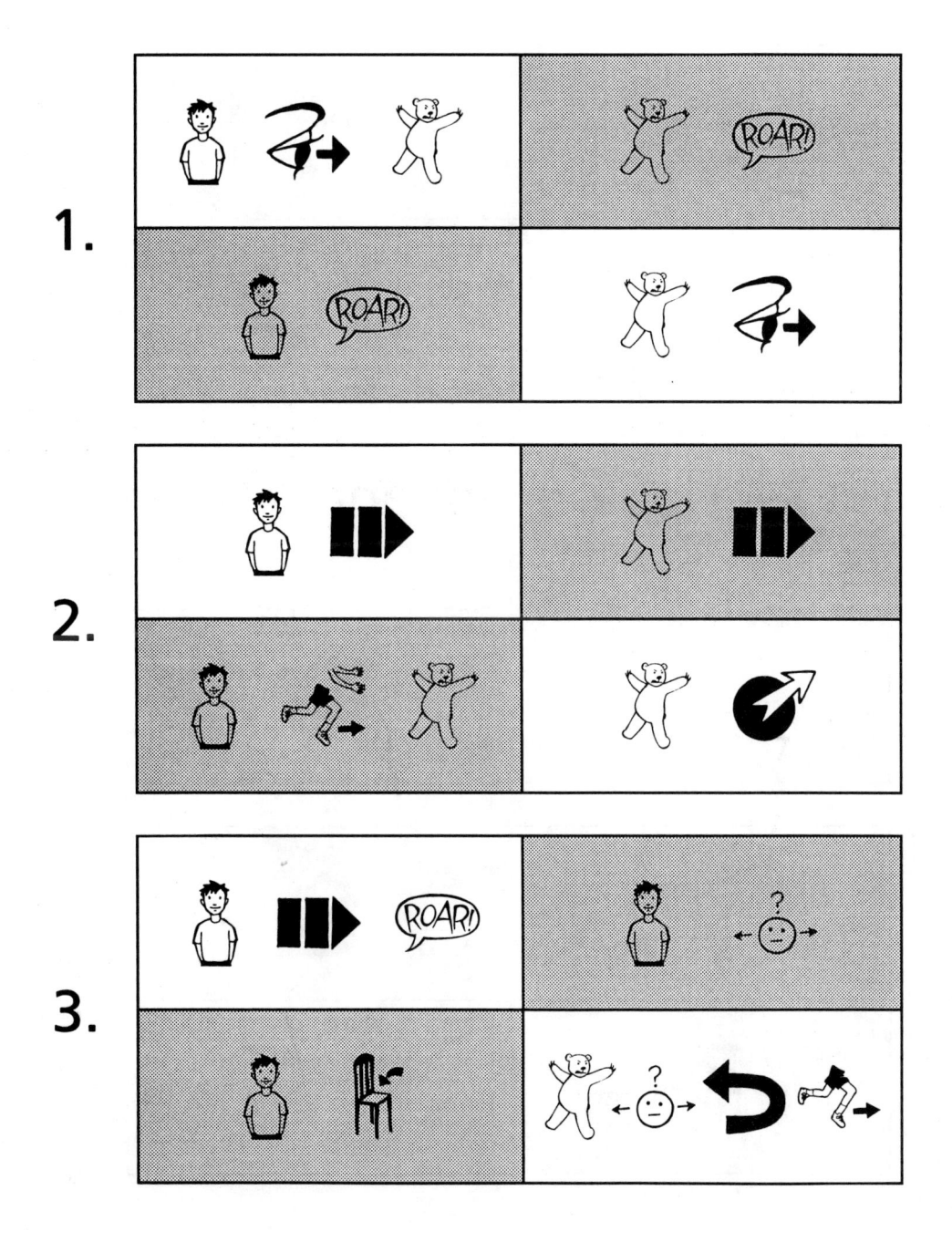

2.

3.

45

Match and Learn
Point to what you hear

#16

4.

5.

6.

46

Rebus Story
Encuentro Peligroso

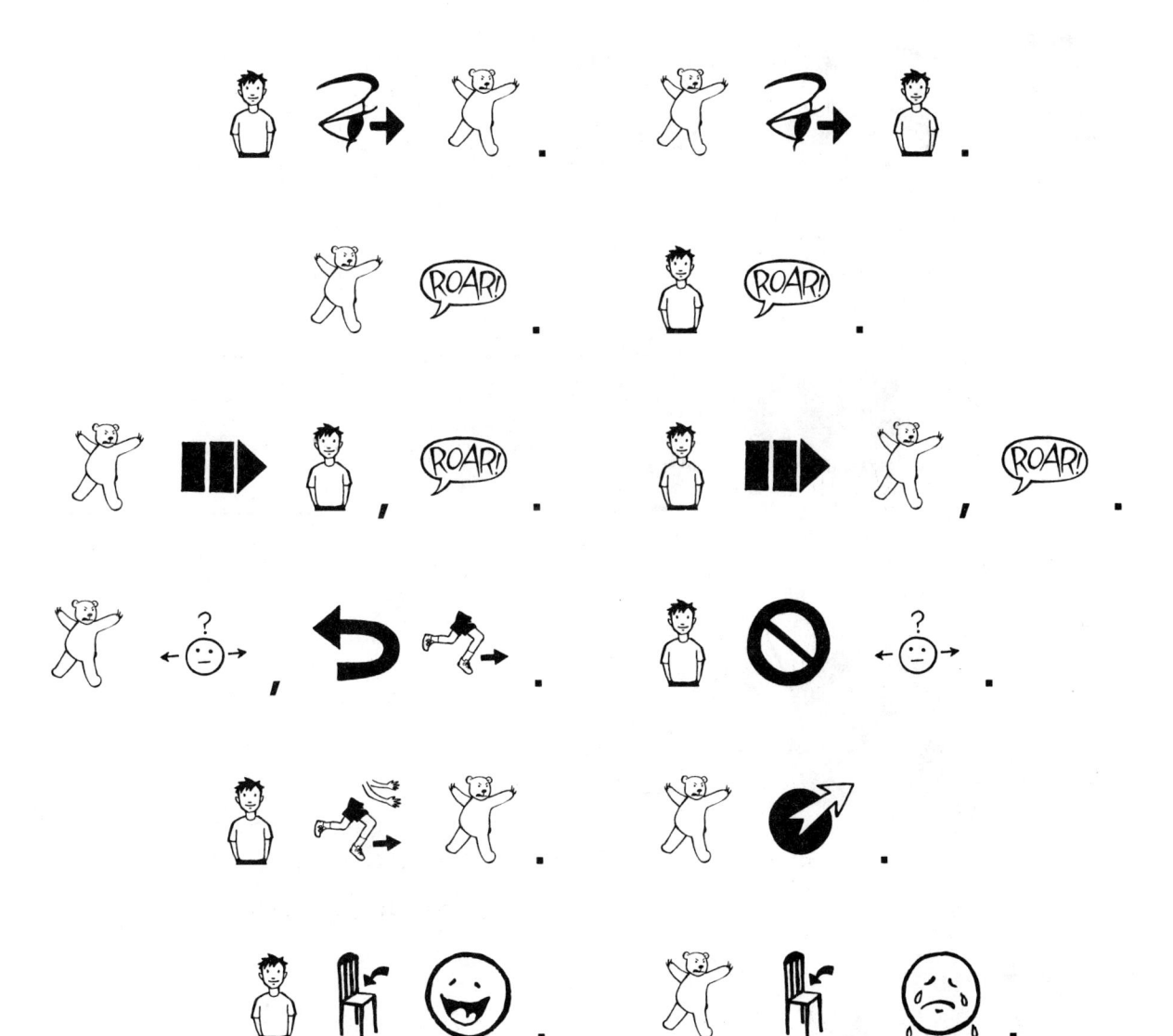

Describe What You See

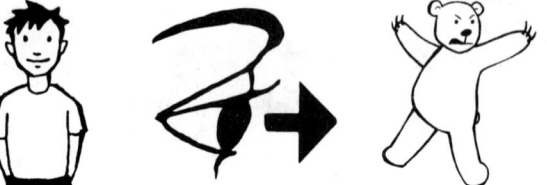

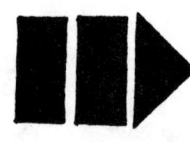

48

Story Telling

Look at the pictures and tell the story

Practice in Spanish
Listen carefully

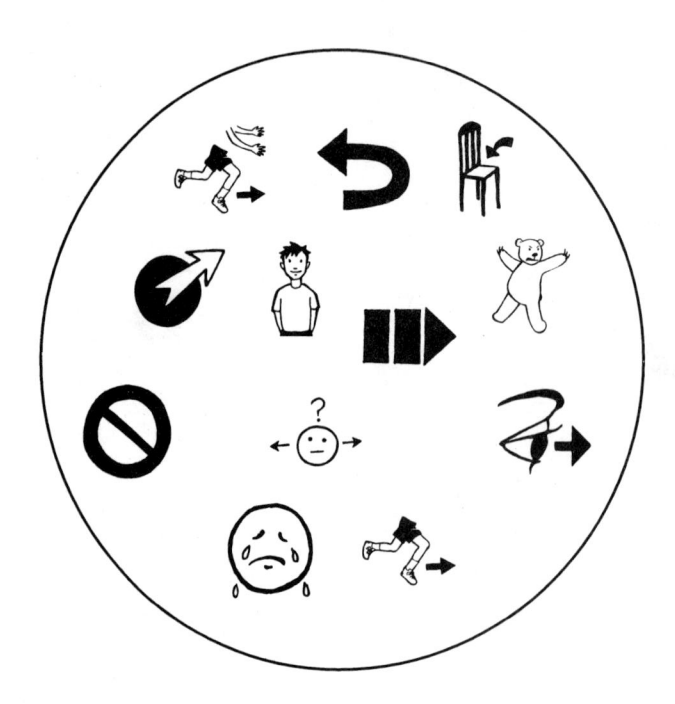

#21, 22

First Time	Fastest Time

The Adventure Continues
At the Market with Marcela

51

Color and Learn
Color the sodas at the market

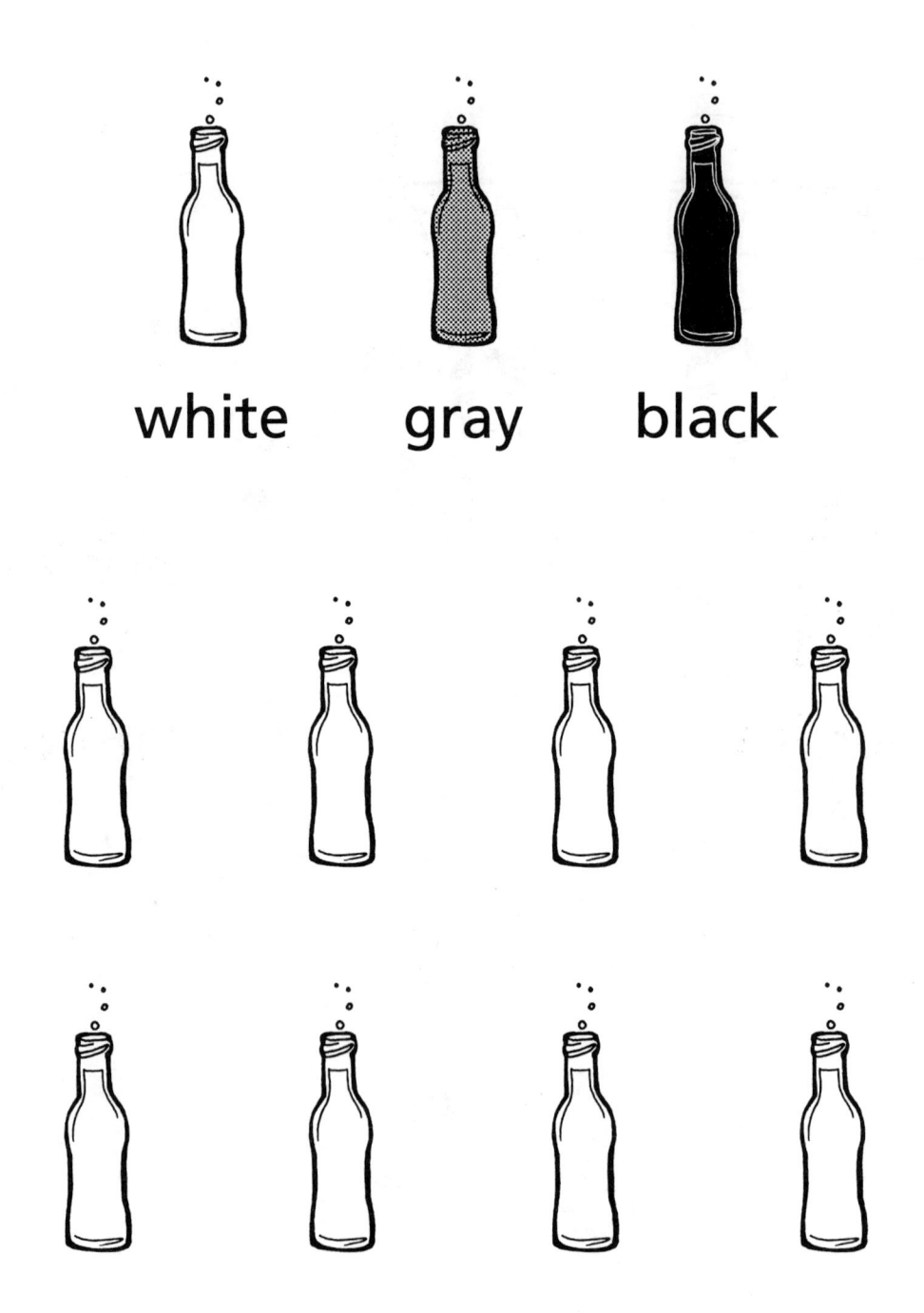

#24

white   gray   black

52

Scatter Chart
Color things found at the market

banana

cherries

lettuce

water

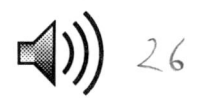

Match and Learn
Point to what you hear

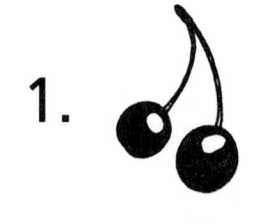

1. 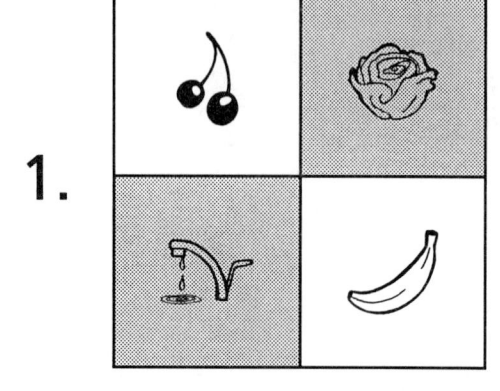
2. 
3. 
4.

1.
2. 
3. 
4.

Scatter Chart
Color things found at the market

grapes

flower

carrot

potato

Match and Learn
Point to what you hear

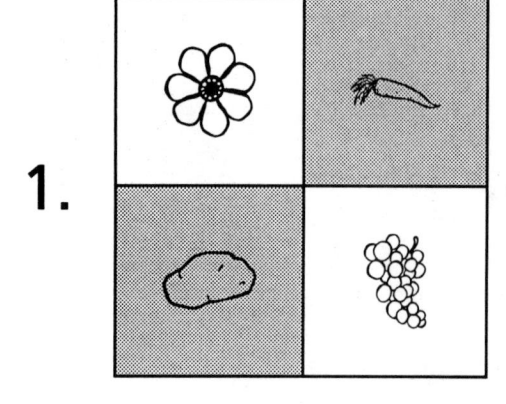

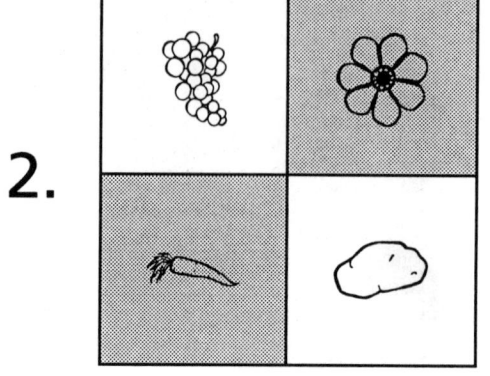

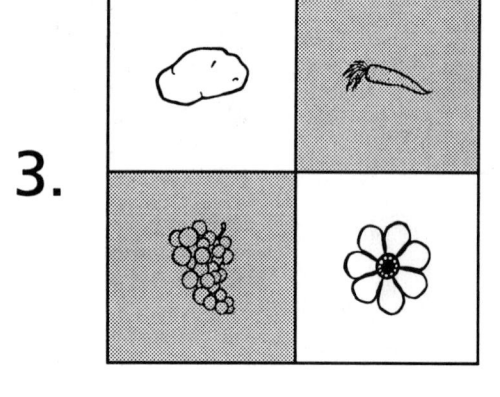

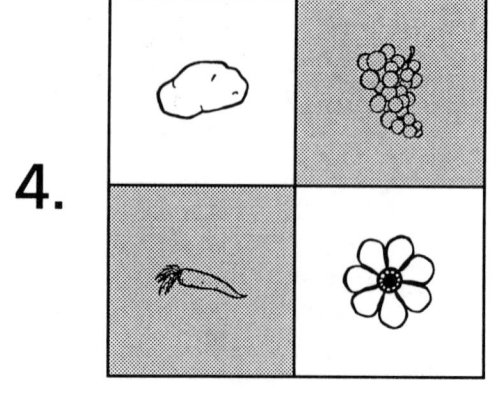

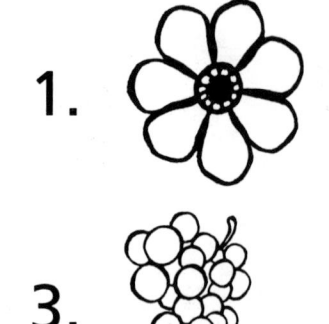

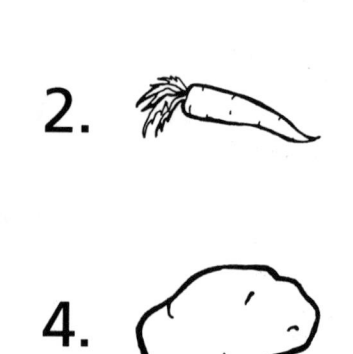

1.
2.
3.
4.

1.
2.
3.
4.

Match and Learn
Point to what you hear

1. 
2. 
3. 
4.

1.  2.  3. 
4.  5.  6.

57

The Adventure Continues
Trek to the Middle of the Island

Un Cuento
The Farmer and the Turnip

Match and Learn
Point to what you hear

1.
2.
3.
4.

1. 2. 3. 4.

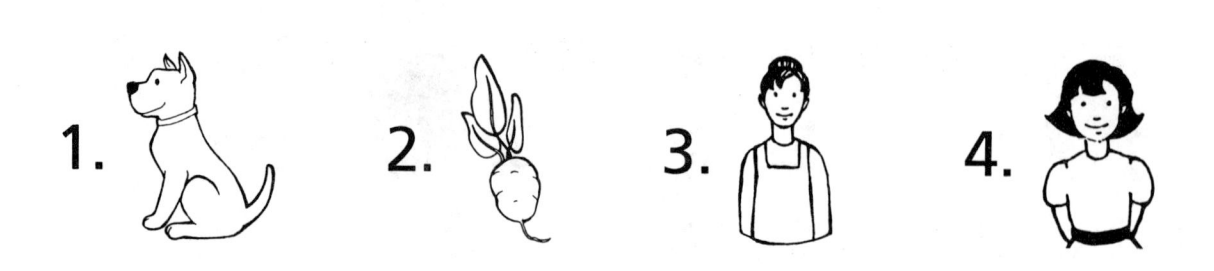

5.

6.

7.

1. 2. 3. 4.

Diglot Weave
The Farmer and the Turnip

Once there was 🧑‍🌾 who planted 🌰. He said: "🌱 will grow from *esta* 🌰 and 🌱 will make a nice meal for *mi* 👨 and *mi* 👩 and me." 🧑‍🌾 Sprinkled water on the ground where he had planted 🌰 and the sun shone and after a few days, a little 🌿 appeared.

And he sprinkled water on the little 🌱 and the sun shone, and 🌱 grew and grew. Every day he sprinkled water on 🌱 and every day the sun shone, and every day 🌱 grew and grew.

After many days 🌱 was very big. And 👨‍🌾 said: "I think 🌰 is ripe."

So he took hold of 🌱 and he tried to pull it out... but 🌰 didn't come out.

So 👨‍🌾 called his 👩‍🍳 : "👩‍🍳, come here. 👩‍🍳, come and help me." And so 👩‍🍳 came to help. She took hold of 👨‍🌾 and 👨‍🌾 took hold of 🌱 and they pulled and pulled… but 🌰 didn't come out.

So 👨‍🌾 called his 👧 : "👧, come here. 👧, come and help us." And so 👧 came to help.

She took hold of 👩 and 👩 took hold of 👨‍🌾 and 👨‍🌾 took hold of 🌱, and they pulled and pulled… but 🌰 didn't come out.

So they called 🐕 : "🐕, come here. Come and help us." So 🐕 came to help.

🐕 took hold of 👧 y 👧 took hold of 👦 y 👦 took hold of 👨‍🌾 and 👨‍🌾 took hold of 🌱 and they pulled and pulled… but 🌰 didn't come out.

So 👨‍🌾 called 🐱: "🐱, come here 🐱. Come and help us." So 🐱 came to help.

🐱 took hold of 🐶 y 🐶 took hold of 👧 y 👧 took hold of 👦 y 👦 took hold of 👨‍🌾 y 👨‍🌾 took hold of 🌱, and they pulled and they pulled… but 🌰 didn't come out.

At that moment, a little mouse, a little 🐭 came by and 🐭 said: "Hey, what's going on here?"

And 🧑‍🌾 explained: "We pull and we pull, but 🥕 won't come out." Then the little 🐭 said: "Maybe I can help." At first they all laughed at him: "Ha ha ha ha. You're so little. How can you help us?" But 🐭 said: "Well, we can all at least try one more time."

And so 🐭 took hold of 🐱, y 🐱 took hold of 🐶, y 🐶 took hold of 👧, y 👧 took hold of 👩, y 👩 took hold of 👨‍🌾, y 👨‍🌾 took hold of 🌱, y they pulled y they pulled y... guess what happened? 🥕 came out.

Just think, from that tiny little 🌱 that 👨‍🌾 planted, with plenty of water y plenty of sun, a big 🌿 and a giant 🥕 grew. Y for ten days 🐀, y 🐱, y 🐕, y 👧, y 👩, y 👨‍🌾 ate 🥕. Nothing remained save one tiny little 🌱.

Match and Learn
Point to what you hear

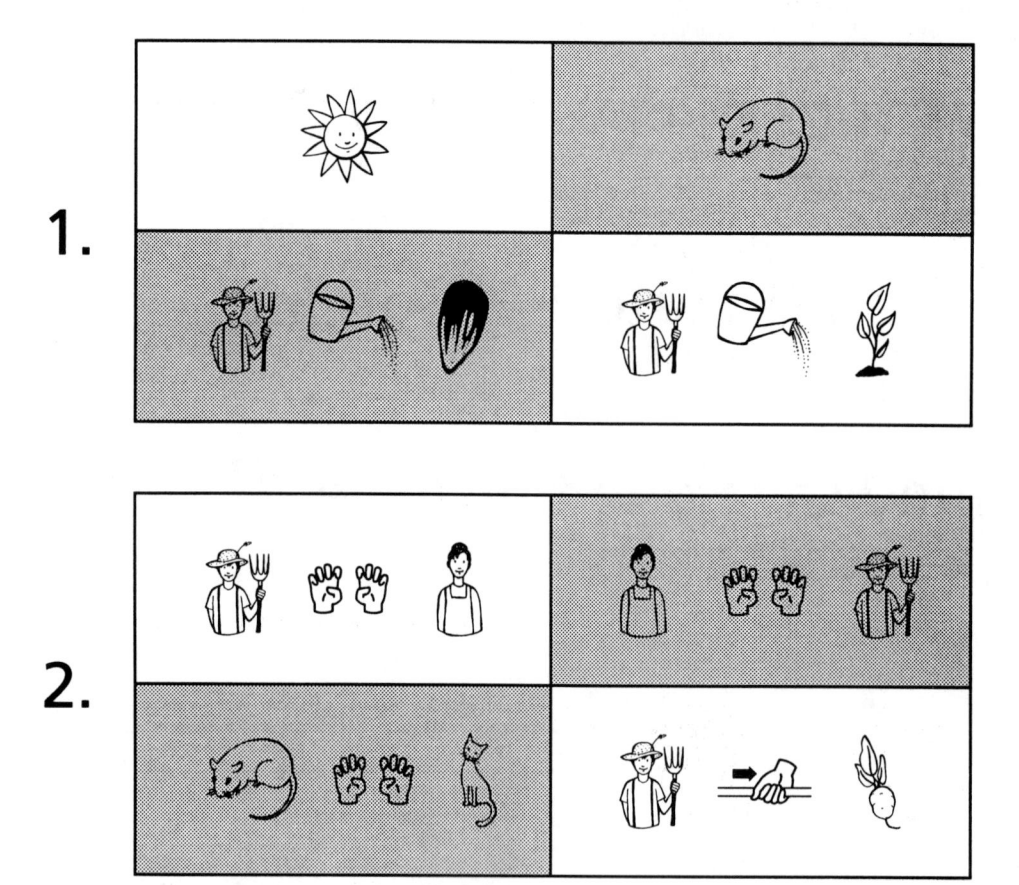

1.

2.

72

Describe What You See

_____

_____

_____

_____

_____

73

Story Telling

Look at the pictures and tell the story

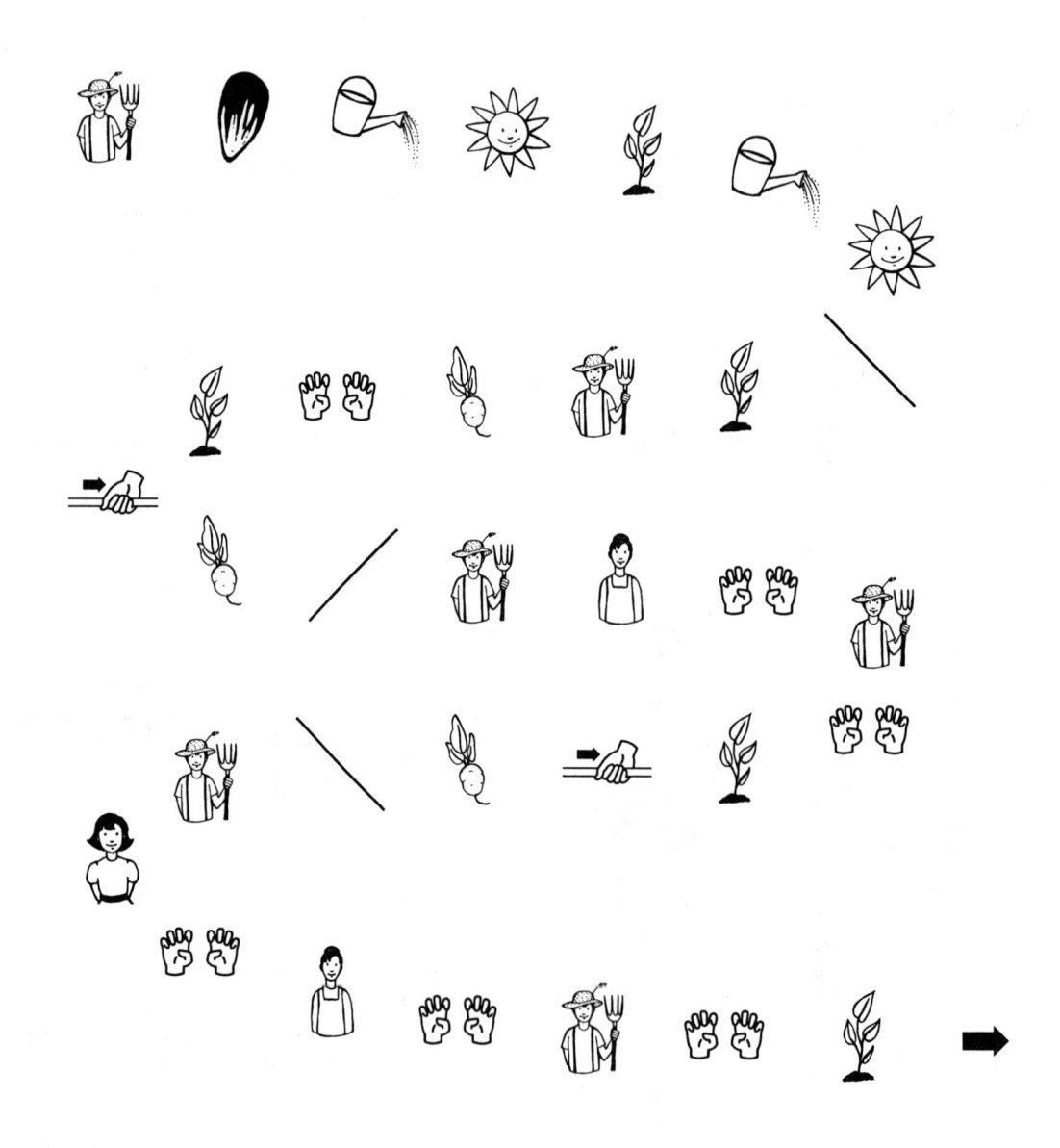

74

Story Telling
Look at the pictures and tell the story

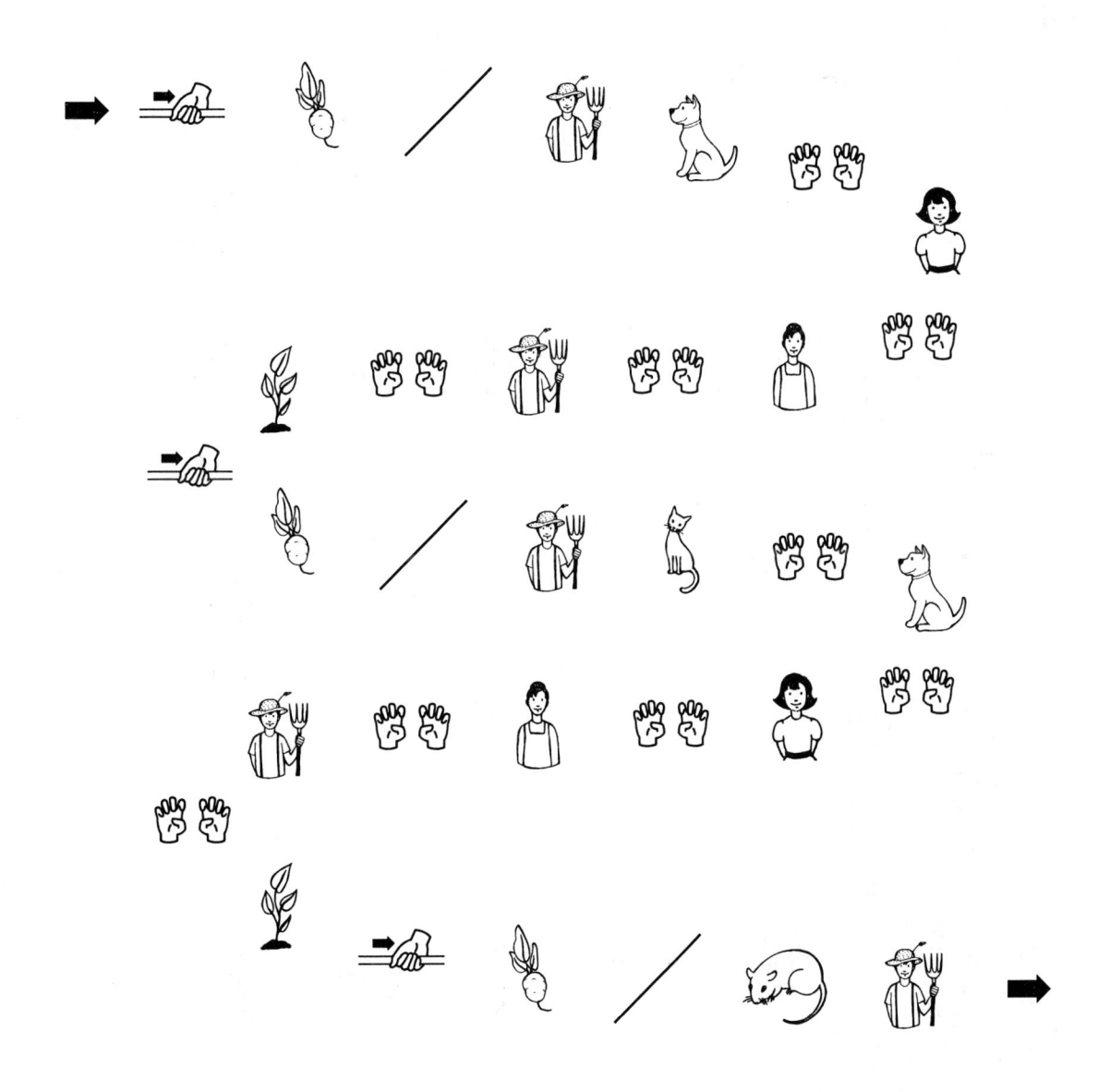

Story Telling
Look at the pictures and tell the story

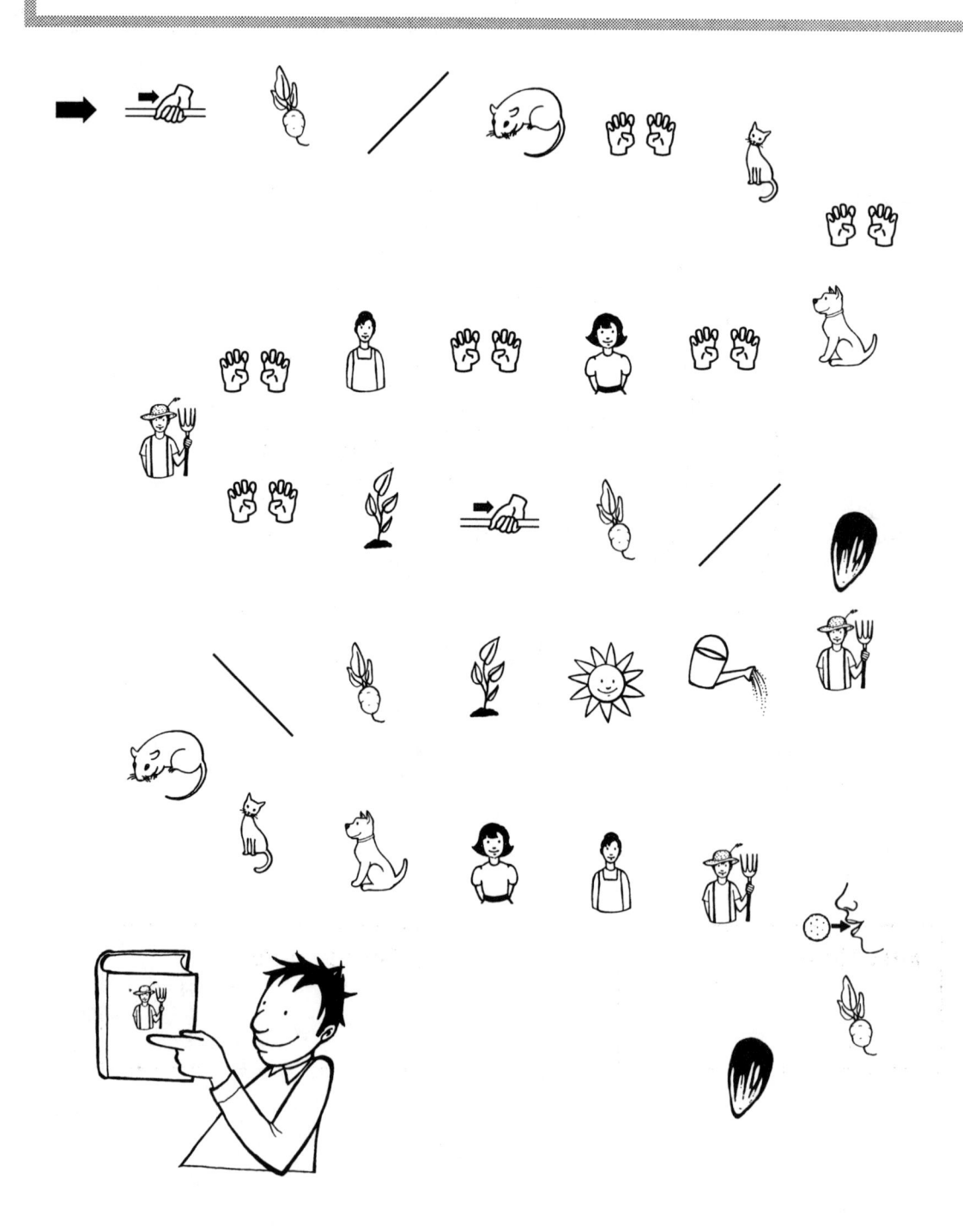

Practice in Spanish
Listen carefully

First Time	Fastest Time

The Adventure Continues
Party with Javier

Story Telling
The Keys to the Gates of Rome

Scatter Chart
Point to what you hear

plaza

perico

casa

calle

señorita

cama

llaves

81

Follow Along
Point to what you hear

Estas son las llaves de Roma.
¡Tómalas!
En Roma hay una plaza.
En la plaza hay una calle.
En la calle hay una casa.
En la casa hay una cama.
En la cama hay una señorita.
A los pies de la señorita hay un perico.
Y el perico dice,
«¡NO DIGAS MENTIRAS!»
La señorita no está en la cama.
La cama no está en la casa.
La casa no está en la calle.
La calle no está en la plaza.
La plaza no está en Roma.
Y éstas llaves no son las llaves de Roma.
¡Perico loco!

Practice in Spanish
Look at the picture and tell the story

The Adventure Continues
Meeting Constancia

Body Parts

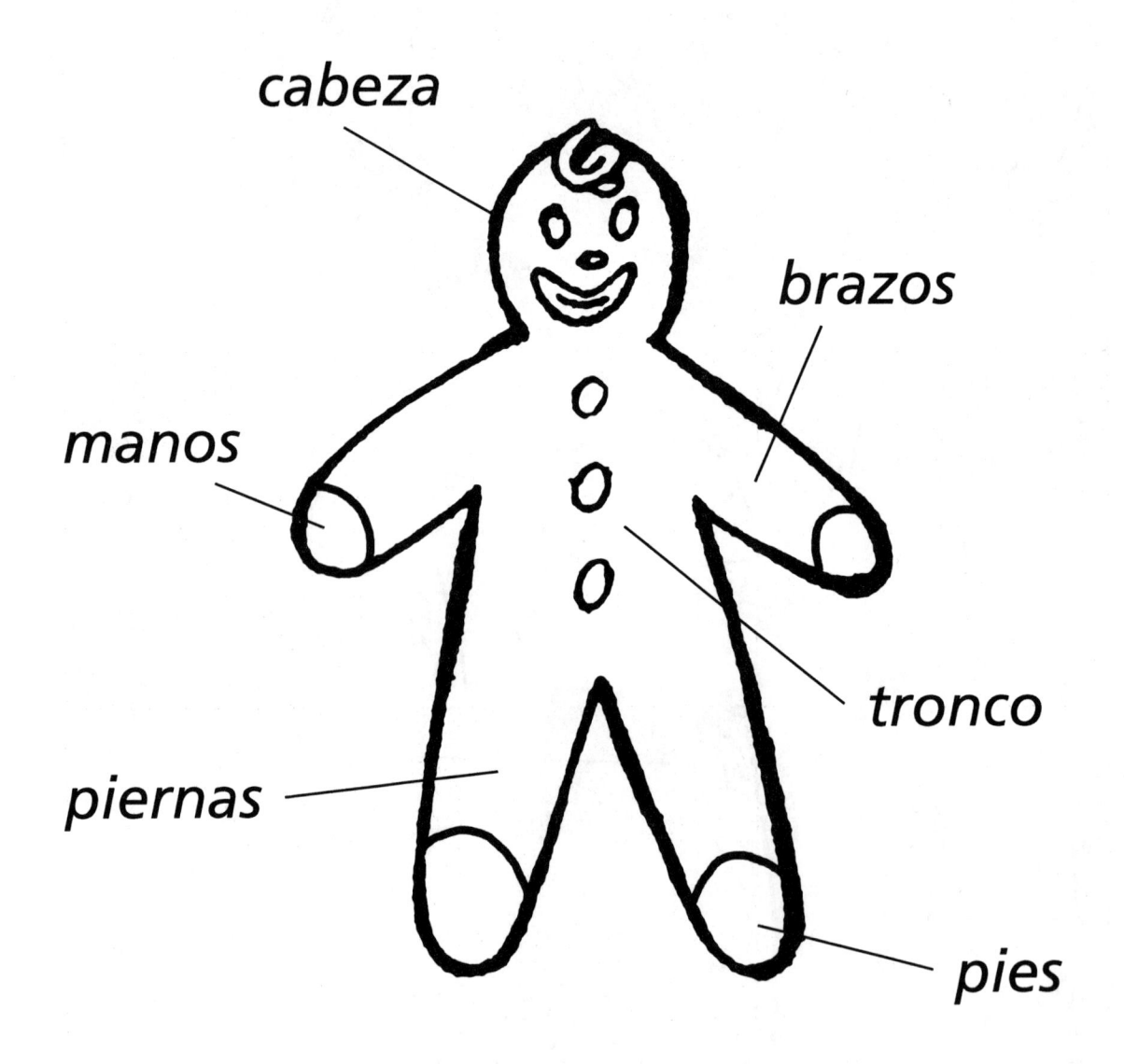

- cabeza
- brazos
- manos
- tronco
- piernas
- pies

Match and Learn
Point to what you hear

87

Draw and Learn
Draw what you hear

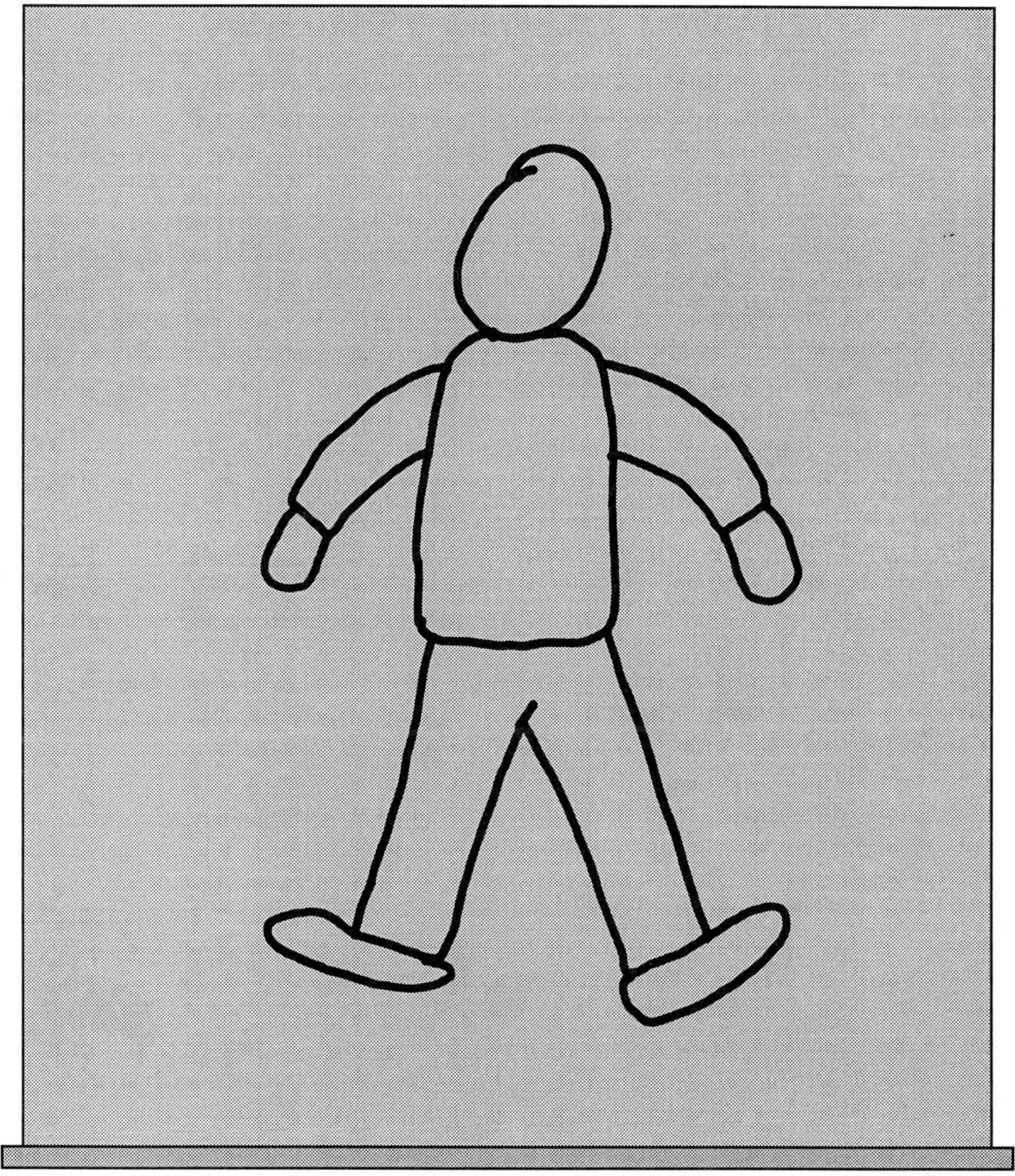

Match and Learn
Point to what you hear

1. 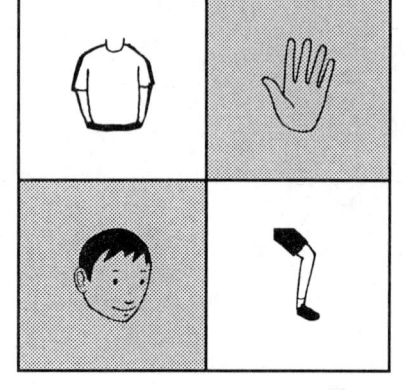
2. 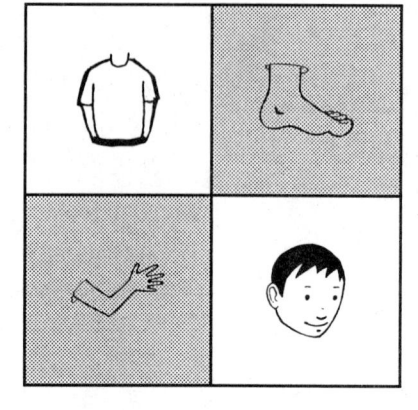
3. 
4.

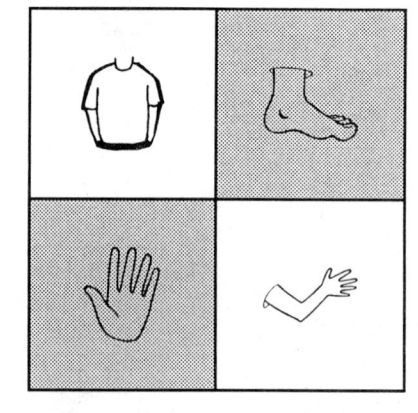

1. 
2. 
3. 
4. 
5. 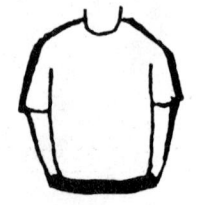
6.

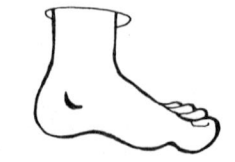

Draw and Learn
Trace your hand

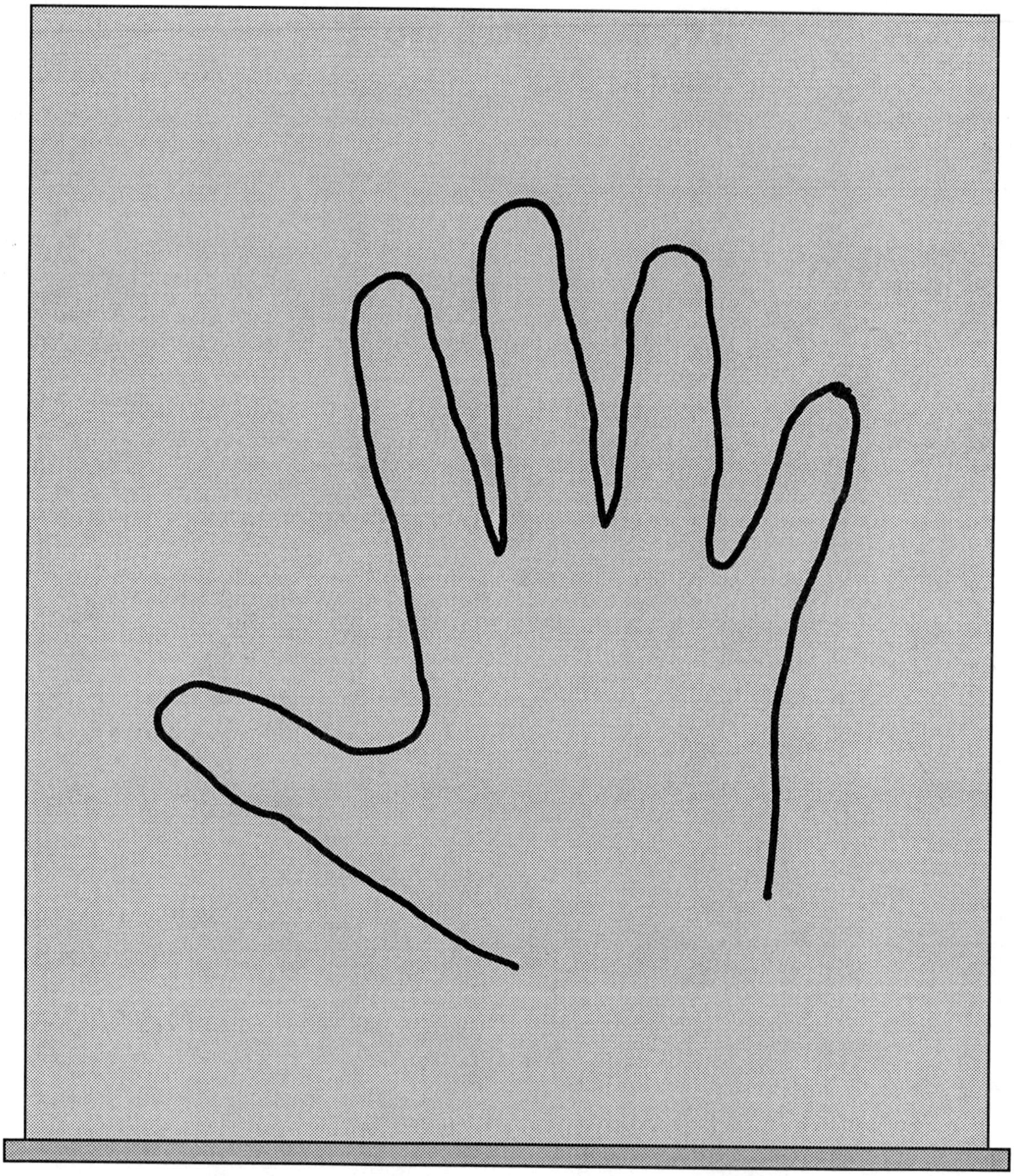

Face Parts

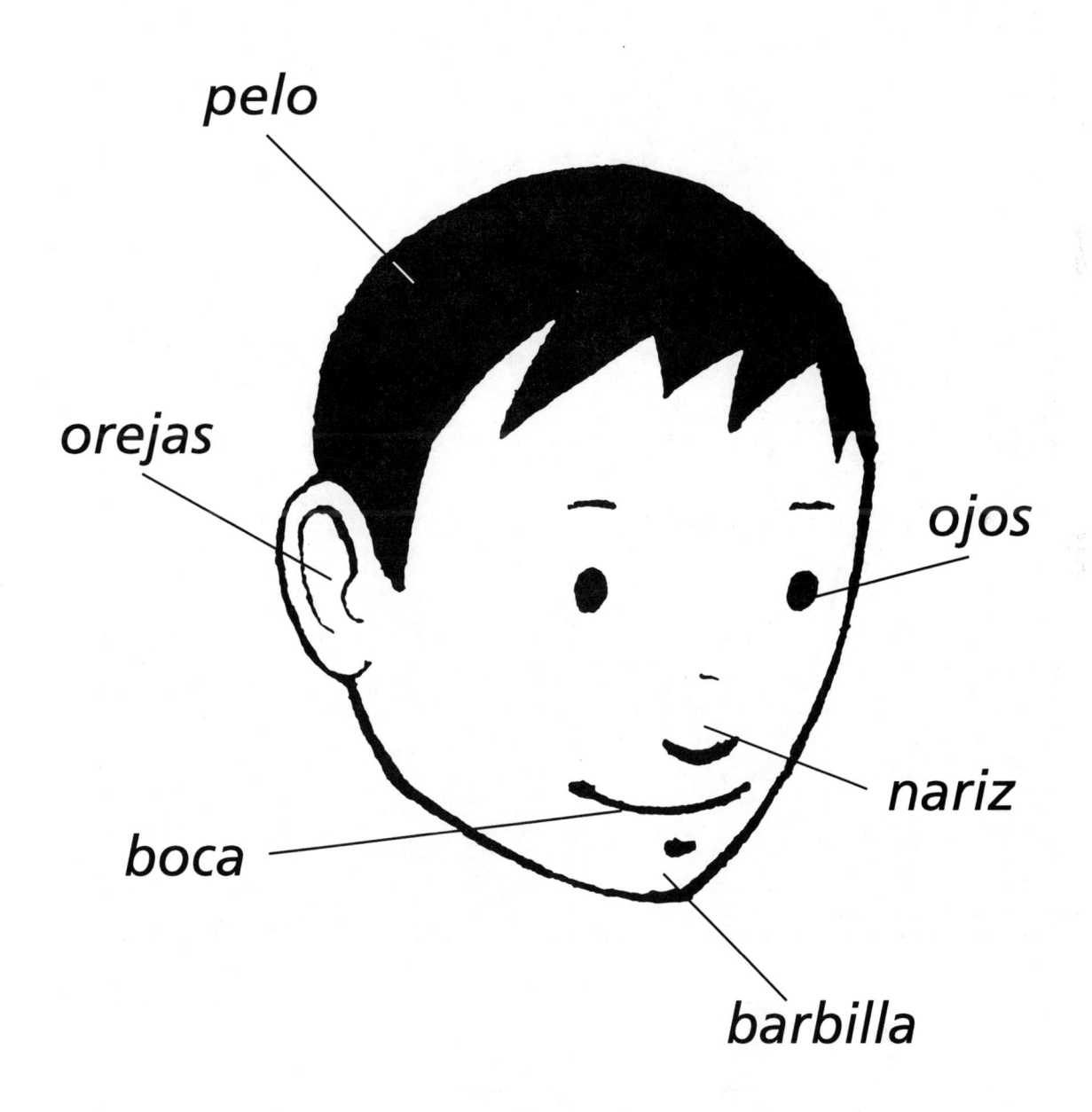

- *pelo*
- *orejas*
- *ojos*
- *nariz*
- *boca*
- *barbilla*

Draw and Learn
Draw what you hear

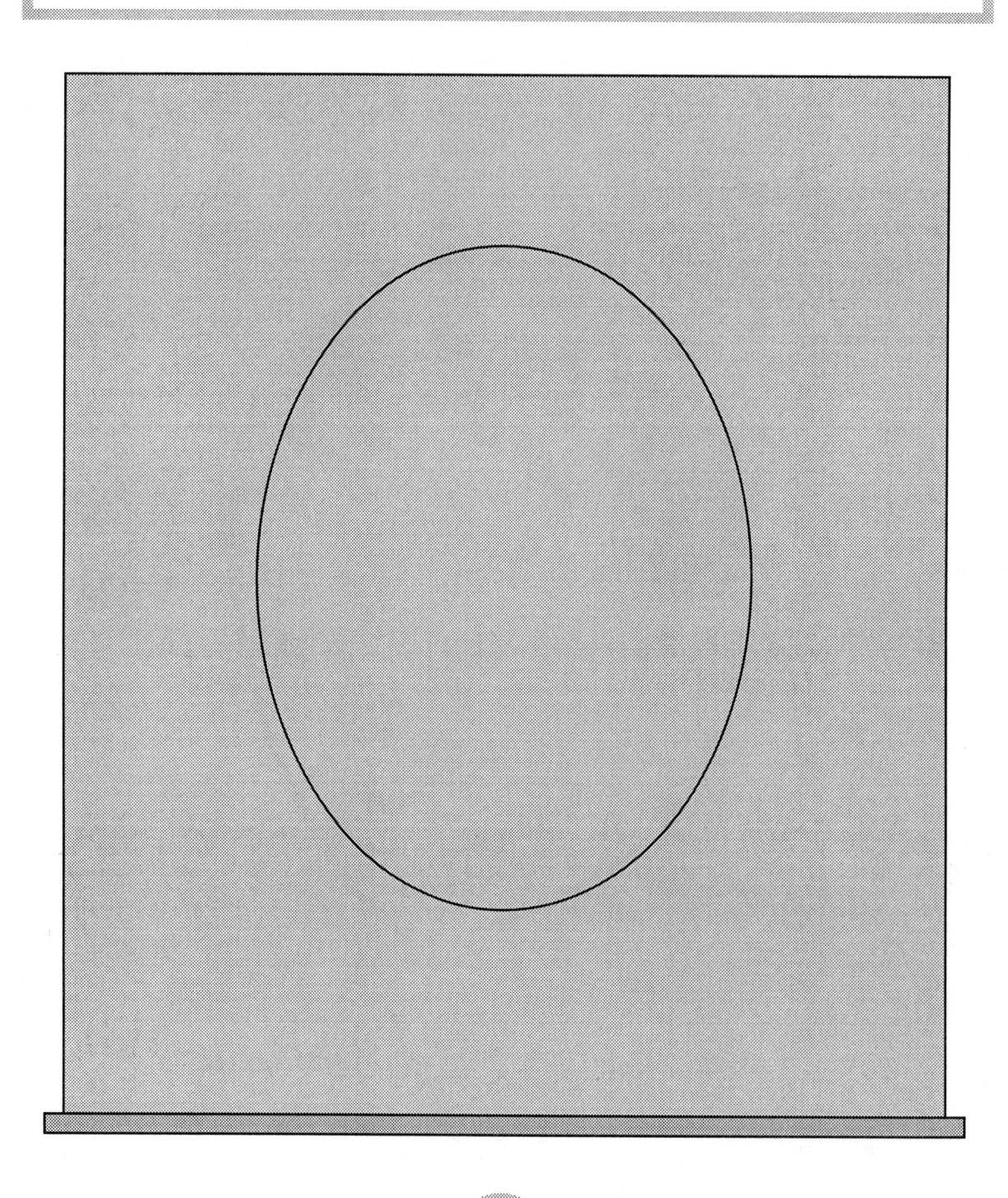

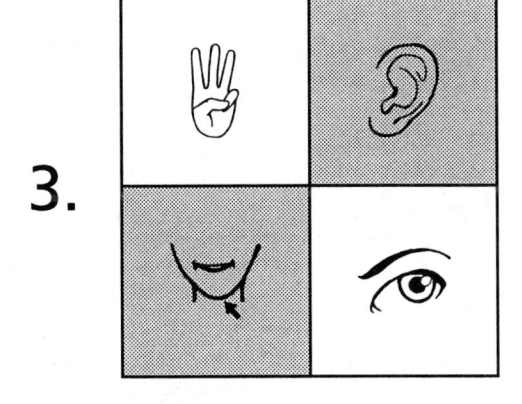

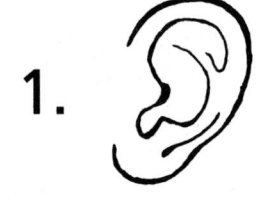

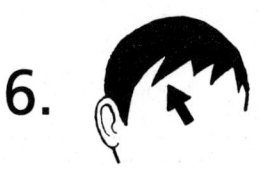

Match and Learn
Point to what you hear

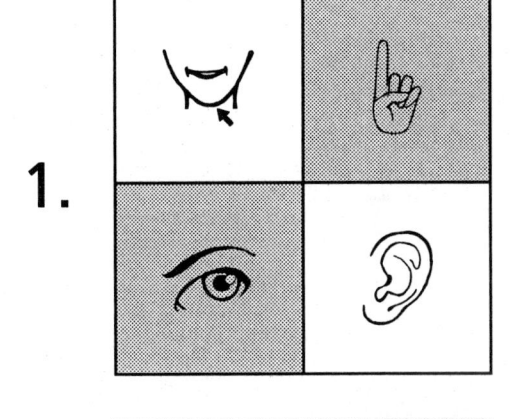

1.
2.
3.
4.

1. (ear)
2. (eye)
3. (chin)
4. (nose)
5. (mouth)
6. (hair)

Touch and Learn
Touch what you hear

1. *Nariz*

2. *Brazos*

3. *Pies*

4. *Tronco*

5. *Boca*

6. *Barbilla*

7. *Manos*

8. *Orejas*

9. *Pelo*

10. *Piernas*

Sing and Learn
Do the actions as you sing

Cabeza, hombros, tronco, pies,

tronco, pies, tronco, pies,

Cabeza, hombros, tronco, pies,

Ojos, orejas, boca y nariz.

The Adventure Continues
Listening to Esmeralda's Story

Diglot Weave
The Broken Window

Match and Learn
Point to what you hear

1. 
2. 
3. 
4. 
5. 
6.

Match and Learn
Point to what you hear

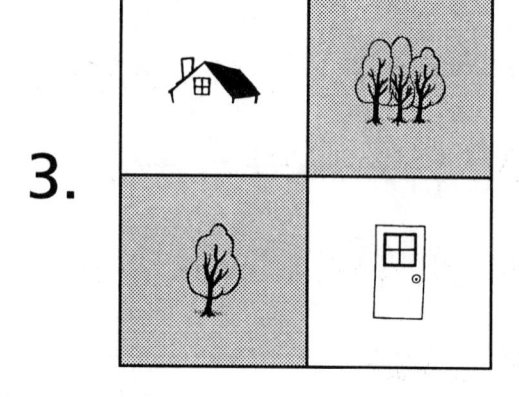

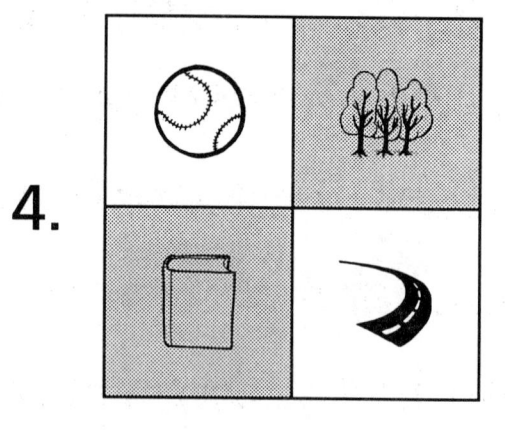

1.
2.
3.
4.

> # Diglot Weave
> ## The Broken Window

The Broken Window—*La Ventana Rota:* A *Cuento* about a Smashed *Ventana*

Would you like me to tell you *un cuento*? *Oquei*, let me tell you *un cuento* about some naughty *muchachos*—some *muchachos y* some *muchachas*—who were playing with a ball in *la calle* near *una casa*.

In this *dibujo* you can see *la casa*. *Mi cuento* concerns *estos muchachos, la pelota* that they are playing with, *y una* glass *ventana* on *la segunda* story *de la casa*.

Besides being about some *muchachos* playing *pelota en la calle* near *una casa* with glass *ventanas*, this *cuento* is about *un hombre* who is the owner *de la casa*. This *hombre* is not out *en la calle* with *los muchachos*. No.

He is *en* his *casa* when *el cuento* begins. I can tell you now, *el hombre en la casa* gets *muy enojado* at *los muchachos*. Maybe I had better describe *el hombre* to you. You see, *el hombre es muy alto*. He is *tres* meters *alto* and weighs four hundred pounds. *El es un gigante, un gigante* like Goliath *en la Biblia*.

Here is *un dibujo* of *el gigante* who is *el* owner *de la casa*. Look at his *manos* and his *pies*, how *grandes* they are.

Look at his *brazos* and his *piernas*, how *largos* they are. *Su cabeza* is as *grande* as a Texas watermelon. Look at *el gigante: su cara, su boca, su nariz*, how *grandes* they are.

In the beginning of *el cuento*, some little *muchachos* and *muchachas* are playing *pelota en la calle* near *esta casa*.

Probably they shouldn't be playing *pelota en la calle* near *la casa*, but not all *muchachos* are aware of what can happen.

As you might guess, one *de los muchachos* hits *la pelota*, and *la pelota* sails up high *en el aire*. *En este dibujo* you can see *la pelota* up in *el aire*. I think you know what's going to happen.

But before continuing *mi cuento*, let me describe some of the features *de la casa*. You can see them in *este dibujo*. *La casa tiene una puerta. Esta es la puerta*. Of course, almost every *casa tiene* at least *una puerta*. Have you ever seen *una casa* that didn't have *una puerta*?

When you leave your *casa*, do you usually go out *la puerta*, or do you open *una ventana* and crawl out?

Back to some of the features *de la casa*. *La casa tiene un* roof, *un techo*. *Naturalmente el techo* is on top *de la casa. Este es el techo de la casa*. You might have *visto una casa* without *una puerta*, and you might have *visto una casa* without *una ventana*, but you *probablemente* haven't *visto una casa* without *un techo*.

What usually sticks up out of *un techo*? *Correcto, una chimenea*.

Y, sure enough, sticking up out of *el techo de esta casa es una chimenea. Ésta es la chimenea*, and you see black *humo* billowing out of it. That's what *chimeneas* are for—to let *el humo* out into *el aire*.

You wouldn't want your *casa* to fill up with *humo*, would you? The *humo* would *probablemente* choke you and would surely blacken the inside of *la casa*.

Does *una chimenea* serve any other purpose than to let *el humo* out *de la casa* into *el aire*? Does it make *una casa* look pretty? Can you enter *una casa* through *la chimenea*?

What other things does *la casa tiene* besides *puertas, un techo, y una chimenea* sticking out of *el techo*? Well of course, *la casa tiene ventanas*. From what you can see *en este dibujo, la casa tiene dos ventanas* on *la segunda etapa*.

To review then, *esta casa tiene una puerta, un techo con una chimenea*, billowing out of which is black *humo, y naturalmente la casa tiene ventanas—dos ventanas* that you can *ver, dos ventanas* on *la segunda etapa*.

If you could look through *esta ventana*, you could *ver* something inside. You could *ver* that there is *un hombre* sitting at *la ventana*. And he's holding something *en sus manos*. It's a *libro*.

He is reading *un libro*.

Who is *este hombre*? *Él* is none other than the *dueño de la casa*, who plays a role *en el cuento.*

Other details we need to mention. Growing near *la casa* is *un árbol*. And hanging from a limb *del arbol* is an apple, *una manzana*. On the other side *de la calle* is a forest, *un bosque*.

Now you know that danger lurks *en el bosque*, but sometimes *los muchachos* forget about danger.

Well now, what will happen? *¿Qué piensas tú? ¿Piensas que la pelota* breaks *la puerta*?

No, la pelota no rompe la puerta. ¿Piensas que la pelota lands on *el techo? No, la pelota no aterriza en el techo.*

¿Piensas que la pelota deciende through la chimenea? No, la pelota no deciende por la chimenea. ¿Piensas que la pelota crashes through la ventana? Exactamente eso es lo que pasa. La pelota crashes por la ventana y hits the gigante right in his nariz…ay ay.

Now, ¿qué piensas que va a pasar? Piensas que los muchachos will run away? Piensas que el hombre, el dueño de la casa, will punish them?

Piensas que los muchachos will have to *pagar* the cost of *la ventana*?

Escucha bien to the *continuación del cuento.* When *la pelota* breaks *la ventana y* smacks the *gigante* on his *nariz, él* jumps up *y* looks out *la ventana. Él ve a los muchachos. O él* is *enojado, muy enojado.* Why?

¿Por qué is *el hombre enojado*?

Well, wouldn't *tú* be *enojado* if *unos muchachos* threw *una pelota y* broke *la ventana de* your *casa*? *Y si la pelota* smacked you right on your *nariz*?

So *¿qué pasa* after that? *Piensas que el gigante* jumps out *de la ventana y* pursues—*persigue*—the naughty *muchachos*? *Piensas que el gigante* climbs up *la chimenea* onto *el techo* and then jumps off?

Bueno, what does *el hombre* really do?

El throws *la pelota* back out *de la ventana y* calls out gruffly, «*¡Muchachos!*» *¿Y qué piensas que los muchachos* do? *¿Piensas que* they pick up *la pelota y* go knock *a la puerta de la casa y* apologize *al dueño*? *¿O piensas que ellos* leave *la pelota* behind *y* run away? *Exactamente eso es lo que hacen. Ellos* start to run up *la calle. ¿Por qué?* They are afraid.

Ellos tienen miedo that *el gigante* will catch them. *Ellos tienen miedo que* they will be punished.

Ellos tienen miedo que they'll have to *pagar el costo de la ventana rota.* ¿*No piensas tú que el hombre* has a right to punish the *muchachos*? ¿*No piensas tú que él tiene* the right to make them *pagar por la ventana rota?*

Bueno, to *continuar el cuento*.

As *los muchachos corren* up *la calle* (the highway), *ellos* see a lady, *una mujer*, coming toward them. *La mujer ve a los muchachos* go *corriendo* up *la calle*.

She calls out to them. «*¡Muchachos!* Wait. *¡Espérense!*» *¿Qué piensas que la mujer* wants to do?

Now look at the woods. A close look will reveal something sticking out from under *un árbol*.

There's an arrow—*una flecha*—pointing to it. *Mira. He aquí la flecha*. What could *la flecha* be pointing to? Could it be a tail? Yes, it could be pointing to *una cola*. Could it be *la cola de un lobo*? A big bad *lobo*?

¿Piensas tú que la flecha indica la cola de un lobo? Perhaps a ferocious wolf, *un feroz lobo* is hiding under *un árbol* there *en el bosque*.

Are you afraid *que el feroz lobo* is going to eat *los niños*? *Escucha* closely as *mi cuento* unfolds, *y tú* will find out what *pasa*. After *el gigante* calls out, «¡*Muchachos!*» *los muchachos* don't stop. *Ellos* run off into *el bosque*. *Ellos* are more afraid *del hombre, del gigante*, than they are *del feroz lobo*.

Just as *ellos* enter *en el bosque, ellos* see something hiding behind *un árbol*. Could it be *el feroz lobo*?

Or is it only Bobi, *un* big dog, *un gran perro* that loves to play *en el bosque con los muchachos*? It *no es Bobi*. It *es el feroz lobo. Y el lobo es muy* hungry. Just as *el lobo* charges, *los muchachos* catch sight of *el gran perro que* likes to play *en el bosque con los muchachos.* «¡Bobi! ¡Bobi!» cry *los muchachos*. Bobi comes running, chases *el feroz lobo, y* saves *los muchachos. Bobi es el héroe.*

Los muchachos run out *del bosque.*

Ellos go back to *la casa*, knock *a la puerta, y* offer to *pagar por la ventana rota*.

Now *el hombre no* is angry, *no está enojado. Él dice a los muchachos,* "That's all right. *La ventana rota no importa*. I'm just happy *que el lobo* did not eat you."

The Adventure Continues
Meeting Esteban at the Beach

Match and Learn
Point to what you hear

1.
2.
3.
4.
5.

126

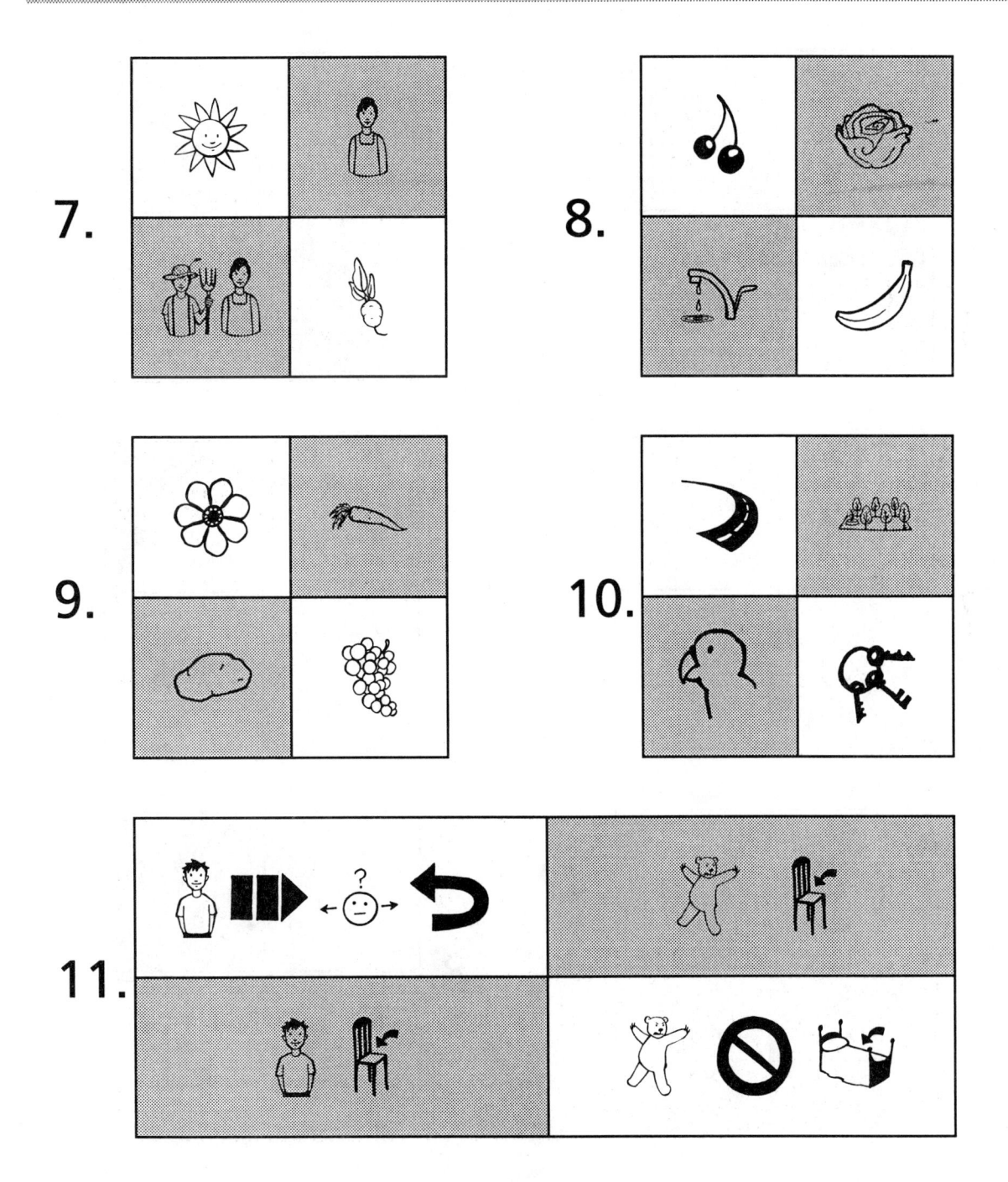

Match and Learn
Point to what you hear

7.

8.

9.

10.

11.

127

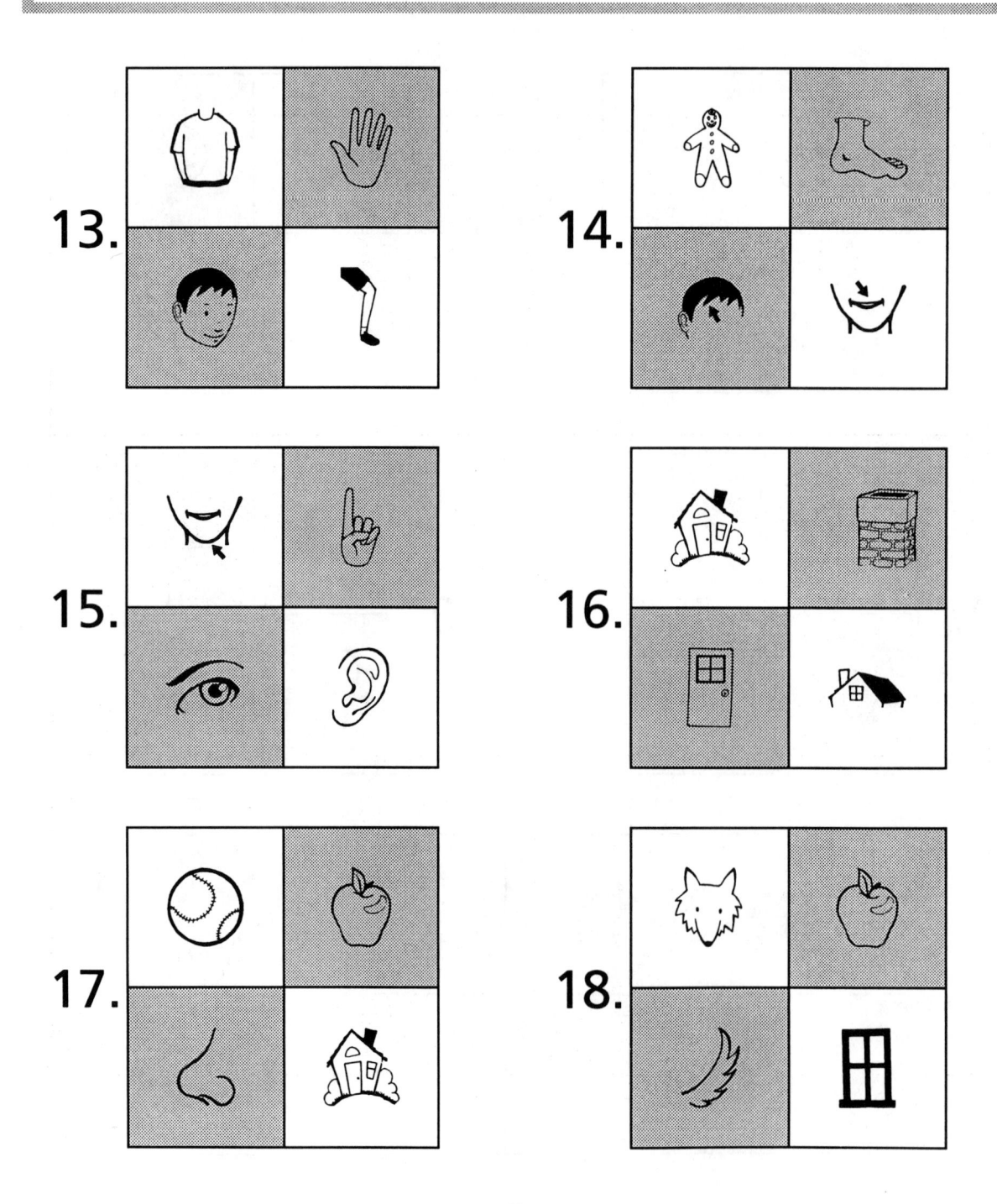

Match and Learn
Point to what you hear

13.
14.
15.
16.
17.
18.

Match and Learn
Point to what you hear

Match and Learn
Point to what you hear

Match and Learn
Point to what you hear

Letter Code
Respond to what you hear

Example:

¿Qué es eso? *Eso es una casa.*

1. ¿Qué es eso? _____

2. Eso es un perro, ¿no? _____

3. ¿Y qué es eso? _____

4. Eso es una niña, ¿no? _____

5. ¿Qué color es eso? _____

Diglot Weave
Esteban's Story

In the jungles of *esta isla*, there are more things than you see at first.

Anywhere you look, there might be something hidden behind (*árbol*), or (*roca*).

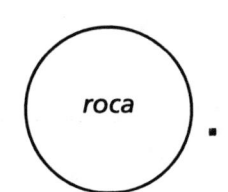

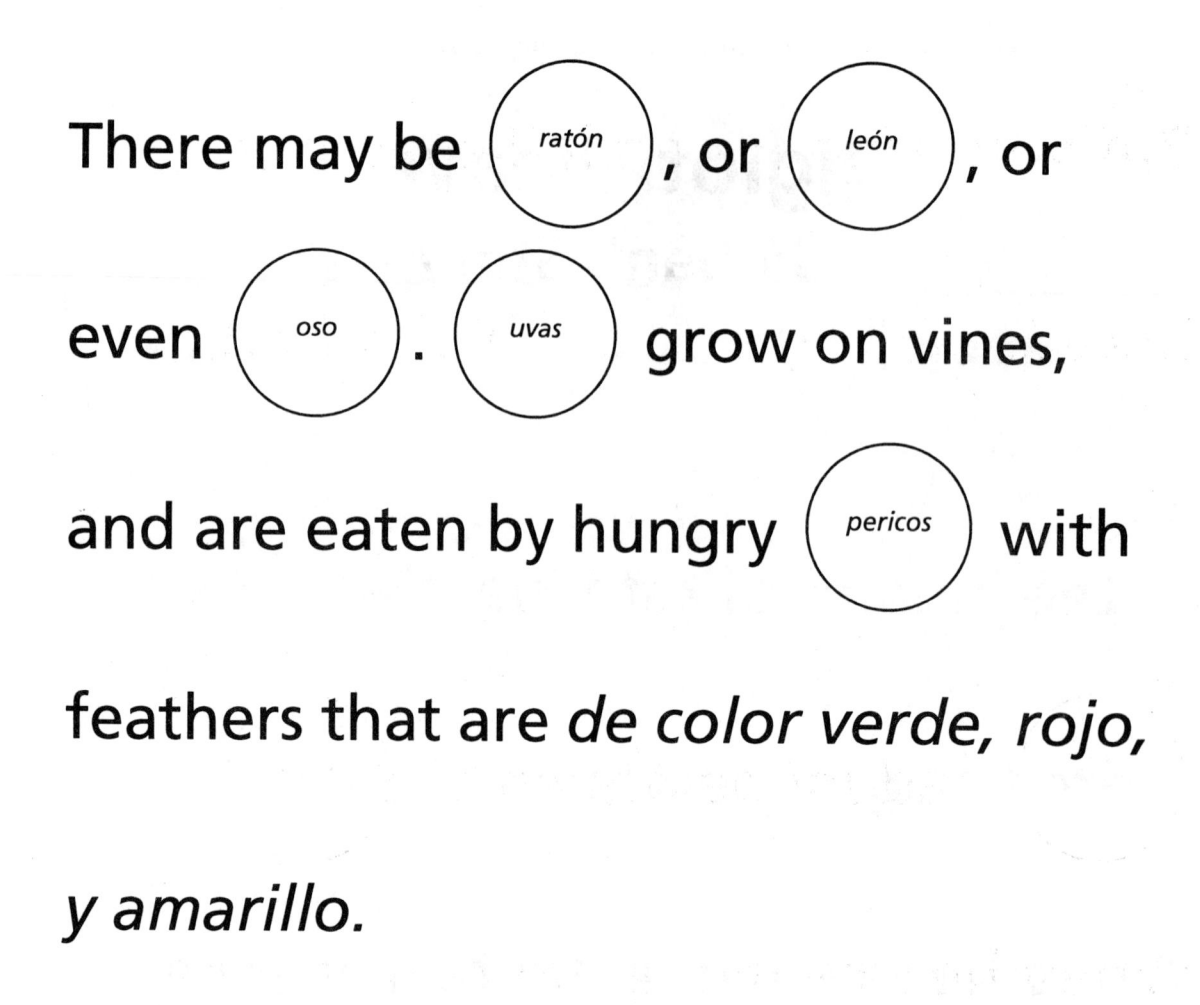

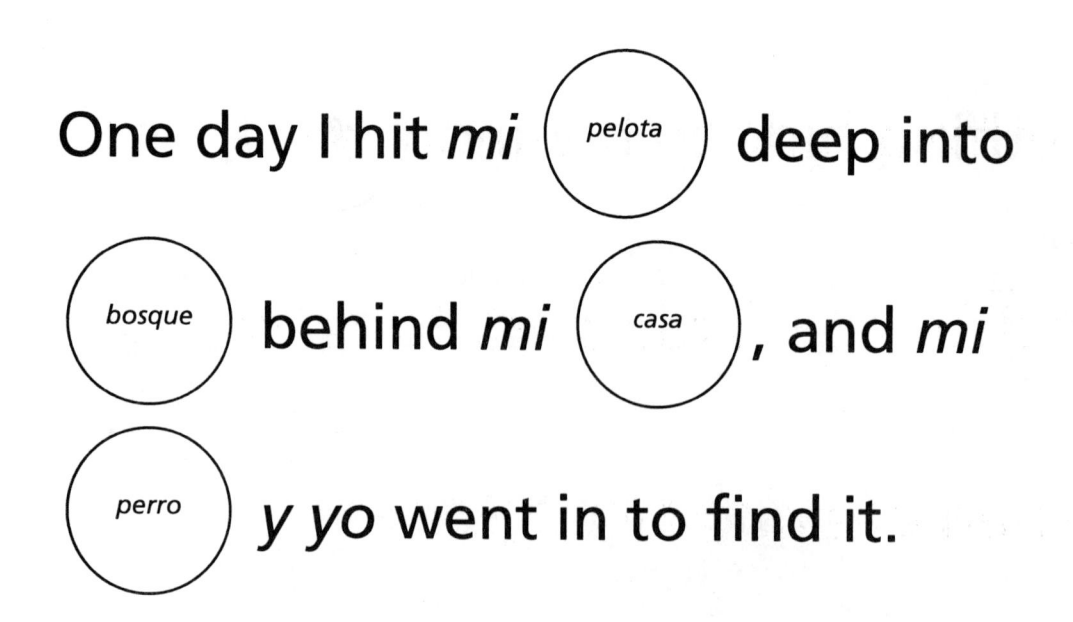

There may be (ratón), or (león), or even (oso). (uvas) grow on vines, and are eaten by hungry (pericos) with feathers that are *de color verde, rojo, y amarillo.*

One day I hit *mi* (pelota) deep into (bosque) behind *mi* (casa), and *mi* (perro) *y yo* went in to find it.

But when we found it, I cried out, because a huge (tigre) had found it first.

(tigre) had *mi pelota en su* (boca).

When he saw me, *el tigre avanzaba* toward me, (rugiendo). I was very frightened, and ran back to *mi casa y* watched *el tigre* through (ventana).

El tigre stood outside *mi* (casa), *rugiendo—rrr!*

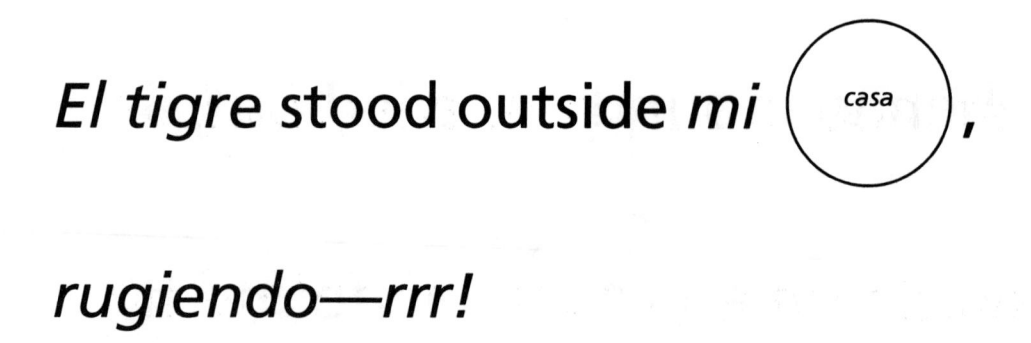

How will I ever get *mi pelota* back from *el tigre*, I wondered? *Mi perro* is good at chasing (gatos) *y* (ratas), but not *tigres!*

Just then, (agricultor) appeared.

As I watched in surprise, *el agricultor* reached down and took *mi pelota* out of *la boca del tigre*. Then he knocked on (*puerta*) *de mi casa y* gave *mi* (*pelota*) back to me. He explained, this is not a wild *tigre* that will eat you up from your (*pies*) to your (*pelo*), but a tame, friendly *tigre*.

It was *rugiendo* at you because it hoped you would come out and play with it!

I could hardly believe what *mis* (*orejas*) were hearing, but it was true! When I went outside *el tigre no me* (*comió*) — didn't eat me!

Instead, it just yawned and then walked over to our bird bath and drank some of (*agua*). And from that day on, almost every day when (*sol*) was shining *mi* (*perro*) and I went into *el bosque* to play with our new *amigo*, (*tigre*).

Draw and Learn
Draw what you hear

Story Telling
Arrange your pictures and tell a story

The Adventure Concludes
A Party of Friends

Pictograph Cut-outs

Pictograph Sticker Page

Cut out the pictographs below for use with "Esteban's Challenge." You may cut out squares along the dashed lines, or if you're daring, cut out the circles. This "sticker" page is intentionally not "sticky" so that you can place the pictograph and double check to make sure its in the right spot before permanently sticking it to the page. When you're ready to permanently affix the pictographs to the page, use double-sided tape or a glue stick. Have fun!